Bismillah With Growth And Development Comes Changes

Felicia Robertson

This book was printed in the United States of America. To order additional copies of this book, contact: Felicia Robertson.

Felicia Robertson

Felicia Robertson

441-8177

www.withgrowthanddevelopmentcomeschange.com

DEDICATION

I dedicate this book to my Children; we have been through a journey that has tested our faith and our loyalty to each other.

To William Elijan Watson, Alante Williamson, Clenest Demon Wells Jr., and the late Starte Leoniece Grace Thomas.

My Children are the center of everything I have become and is yet to be. As I strive to share the Changes in my life from the Streets to The Purpose God has placed on my life, it is my intention to inspire others who have come through a struggle, gang violence, domestic abuse, and family tests and trials to keep striving for God (Allah) is always in control.

Felicia Robertson, aka Magic.

ACKNOWLEDGMENT

I would like to thank many of my supporters and the people that serve this community with honor and dedication.

My thanks go out to the American Culinary Federation, Bridging, Steve Rummler Hope Network, The Waterford, Shingle Creek Neighborhood Association, Al-Maaun, and Imam Macrame. Arthur Hudson Jr, my graphic designer, Ted McNeal, Richard Lofton, Randolph Ellis, Winndye Jenkins Hoover, for her continued support to produce a change in the community.

My sisters Debra Robertson, Dakota Nyaribo, Nail Hobson, and my brother Bobby Lynn Terrell Jr. My cousins Gayle McClain, Tina, and Sheena.

I would also like to thank the Organizational structure and the individuals I have fellowshipped with over the years in the stage of learning to from the cradle to where God shall direct my path in this upcoming future.

A journey is best described as the willingness to prevail despite obstacles and adversity. Overcoming and Becoming a Power to be Reckon with.

Love,

Felicia Robertson.

Table of Contents

FOREWORD

I MET FELICIA ROBERTSON in the Spring of 1992. We were both volunteering for a grassroots political organization known as 21st Century Vote. 21st-century vote stood for voices of total empowerment. Endowed with a Great leader, we were trying to awaken the apathetic sleeping giant in our community, The Black vote.

Not all our peers our age understood the task we had undertaken, but I did, and so did Felicia. I was impressed with her level of understanding of the needs within our communities at such an early age. She definitely was not average or ordinary in any sense of the word, but more importantly, to me anyway, she had a genuine and sincere heart for the people and a hunger to increase in knowledge and experience, all geared toward manifesting into reality the vision of 21st Century vote leadership which was transforming the conditions of the community into a place of integrity, dignity, and opportunity for all.

As I emerged as a young man dedicated to awaking our political power, I began to gather respect and name recognition among my male peers, with the females, the same dynamic was happening with Felicia or Magic as she would come to be known by in the streets. As this dedication continued, it became obvious that Magic and I were now recognized as young leaders at 21st Century

V.O.T.E. What may not have been so obvious is that besides the notoriety we were gaining on the streets, we had both gained the attention of someone we both as well as our community admired greatly...Larry Hoover.

Larry Hoover was the undisputed leader of one of the most infamous street organizations Chicago had ever seen. He was serving 150-200 years in Illinois Department of Corrections for allegedly ordering the killing of another gang member. Larry Hoover, then reported to have been illiterate when he was incarcerated as a young man, had educated himself by taking full advantage of the educational opportunities offered by the D.O.C. He had during his time in prison been very instrumental in helping bring about peaceful resolutions to situations with violent implications between rival inmates but also including correctional staff as well. By the time he began communicating with magic, he had created a new concept call Growth and Development and explored members of the old concept to embrace this new teaching. With no hesitation upon hearing this new concept, magic embraced it and began to conversate regularly with Larry. I'm sure his conversations with her about his vision to help and not harm our community redirected her heart and her life because it certainly did for me...... that's not to say challenges were not on the horizon for magic.... or me.

Experience is the best teacher in life, and oftentimes, despite the best upbringing or advice, sometimes our own decisions lead us down a road towards our own wants and desires. As articulate and intelligent as magic undeniably was, her sudden social status inside the organization led to an irresistible infatuation. A series of questionable decision put her in places and spaces that would break the average person. Yet she endured several crises that could have caused her premature exit from this world. Instead, she emerged from the other side a conqueror with a distinct perspective rooted in wisdom borne from lived experience. She now had a mission, a story to tell, and a desire to live with a purpose, helping others. It has not been easy, life never is. She has again suffered lost and again found purpose in her pain, the uplifting of those living in their pain with the belief there is no hope. Magic is proof positive that there is hope. There is no better example of the resiliency of a woman or testament in the ability to bounce back.

I am both proud and honored to write the foreword here. Magic and I share parallel paths. Both of us share the person who would become and is probably still today the most influential person in each of our lives...Larry Hoover. While some will not consider this a popular thing to say, I am speaking the truth. Without his teachings, I am confident my life would be significantly different and not in an effective way. Today, I am the CEO of a 501c3 not-for-profit agency rooted in Violence Prevention in some of the most disproportionately affected by violence communities in Chicago. Similarly, magic is also heading an organization in Minnesota. I am not sure if, but for her crossing paths with Larry, she would still be doing the work she is. However, I'm confident I would not. I wish magic continued peace and prosperity in her service to others just as she has been groomed to do, knowing as she does that service to others is the purest form of love. ♥

PREFACE

TO GROW AND Develop into the very fabric of God's design for your life may appear to be overwhelming at times. Your faith is often tested, and some outcomes are not always favorable. The experience you encounter prepares you for your next season that Allah has brought you through. You must trust in the Creator to guide you to your purpose.

My text is not a religious book; however, it is the words of truth and an example of how much God's Grace touches our lives even when we know not or think we feel his presence.

The title, With Growth and Development, Comes Change, is an exemplary story of a young girl raised in Chicago and a standing member of the organization known as the GD: s. A group of African American men and women fighting to uplift the voices in their community while learning new innovative ways to legalize their actions and become upstanding citizens. Many of the Men and women have come from poverty-stricken backgrounds, broken homes, domestic violence, and lack of financial stability. This is the beginning of a set of books outlining my tests and trials as I grew to become the power to be reckoned with that Larry Hoover had intended for a group of underprivileged people.

Although my behavior had led to incarceration, it has also led to the development of Changing the world of one situation at a time. Uplifting and Guiding in a true nature that a leader should possess.

Change is inevitable. To never dream is worthless, to refuse to act is selfish. To wither is to die. I am in full bloom. I am a replica of Growth and Development.

GROWING UP IN an unstable and hostile environment made my struggle to understand change an exceedingly difficult one. Family circumstances only added to the dysfunction I had grown accustomed to. Becoming a sister of the struggle gave me a family; meeting Mr. Larry Hoover gave me purpose. I grew intrigued by his advice and his constant dream of Change. A new world where organizations like ours would produce doctors, lawyers, congress people, and, yes, police officers. He wanted us to thrive in the political arena and become a power to be reckoned with. The vision had a blueprint to success. Men of less virtue would come to tear down any light the ole man had given us. The federal government would come and sweep our nation up like trash, strip our leaders and confidants with the excuse that this would cease the violence. Now, today, what I once knew to be home has flourished into a war zone. Unfortunately, there is no one left to blame. The government has shielded Mr. Hoover from the world. So, who sparks the violence now? All propaganda becomes exposed. With purpose and direction, one tries to adhere to laws and policies. Today, the world is full of renegades and people moving without a strategic plan. No compassion for peace; war is real. And this is where my story begins.

My wings have been broken for so long that I have forgotten what being a little girl is like. I have hidden away the tears, forbidden myself to cry. So fearful of the God I do not know. I have convinced myself that even death cares not to look at me. How did I get here?

As children, we build barriers and walls of protection from predators. In this glorious attempt, we separate ourselves from being loved; within this separation, we educate ourselves on sipping from the cup of love but never allowing oneself to truly taste its passion, its purity, or its forgiveness. The branches that keep us whole remain buried beneath the guilt and trickery of this world. There is no trust, love is distant, so no seeds are planted. Nothing will grow. The heart remains barren. Love and compassion are blindsided by jealousy, selflessness, hatred, and lack of the ability to dream outside of the box of broken fables given to the African American community.

As we grow older, we find the religious people we have come to know tend to speak of the word agape. To me, that was bullshit. It would take years for any reasoning or understanding of what agape could mean… Many Christians claim it is one of the highest forms of love, a charity, as I had once read. The love of God for man and of man for God. As a child, where does this connection start? For Muslims, they say it starts at the mother's feet simply because she is the vessel that which life has bloomed through. We assume that this courageous act of birthing would create the unbreakable bond of love. As children, we need this. We are alone within our subconscious; we are fragile and codependent for that nourishment of human affection. But some realities appear far more sinister than others.

Who prepares the child born into a world where she is ushered in as a burden? Many would conceal the statement of accidental birth. So, in shame, the parent would pretend that the love is strong, and the bond is growing stronger by the day. The bond of a mother and a daughter. This unbreakable bond that you soon discover is easily broken during chaos and oppression. The fact that this is the giver of life has no precedence over circumstances. For so many years, I searched my heart and my mind, asking this God that I only imagined, "Where did I fail to not receive love's comfort? Did I lack loyalty, did I not grasp the definition of submission, or did I simply not have the strength to cultivate the dreamless vessels in my seasons?"

I learned quickly that the weak has no place for comfort and shelter when being stalked by a ferocious beast. A beast who is created by pain, hardship, and hatred. These types of beasts appear as the princes to every princess who is trapped by poverty, lack of social skills, and physical abuse. Within the safety of the house of uncertainty, the detached princess begins to develop but not grow, to exist but not live, to simply go through life accepting the bullshit life has offered her. A black eye, a broken nose, a backhand slap, or the tossing around from one man to the next. She has taught herself to cope with the abuse. In her dream state, she remains numb to her own existence. She is a face with no mouth to speak. Her words are silent. This was once my normal way of life. Long before magic ever existed, within the Gangster Disciples laid a girl who could not dream past Englewood. She had accepted that her fate was leading to nowhere fast.

How does a flower waiting to bloom get surrounded by weeds? Why does no one tend to the garden? I was angry for years at my mother. Being so young, it was easy to nurture that emotion, that feeling. It was all I began to know. I was not familiar with love. I know it was not familiar with me. In Ephesians 6:1–3 it says, "Children, obey your parents in the Lord, for this is right. 'Honor your father and mother" (this is the first commandment with a promise), 'that it may go well with you and that you may live long in the land.'"

In the Quran, in 2:83, it says to worship only Allah; treat with kindness your parents and relatives and orphans and those in need. I was not Muslim in my days of Jalal eel. I could not fathom the mere essence of what God was saying. Currently, I was in the world of the people of the book. I had not found acceptance in my life there; I was of weak faith in anything.

As a child, as broken as you are, you love the only person you have grown to know as you begin your journey through life. The mother is responsible for rearing the child in its younger years. I needed my mother. I depended on her strength. I was yet to develop any for myself at such an immature age. I was ten, and I felt that grace had skipped me. I started off loving my mother more than life itself. She once made me smile and made me feel safe. She made me trust her. But now I was not so sure that my mother loved me. How could she? At ten, I discovered what abandonment was, what it felt like, and what disappointment had to offer. The mother-and-daughter bond was easily broken.

My mother had brought the wounded beast into our lives. I watched how she loved and nurtured it, protected it. She had relinquished to this beast her strength and the power to break my will to want to exist in life. What type of monster devours the innocence of a child, and what type of mother sits back and accepts it? I questioned myself over and over, night after night. Did I somehow mislead this beast into thinking I noticed him? Did I not move like a child? Dear God, was this my fault? Was I so cursed that I reeked of a stench that only a beast would lust for?

It was within this brokenness that I soon learned that love had many faces—smiles that were regrets and hugs that were given as a way out. That is what my mother's love began to feel like. To think I once loved my mother enough to try and protect her. That beast threatened to take my mother's life if I told her. I grieved for her, I held my tongue until we got to a safe place, and I did different from most. I told her right away. I cried out for help. But the look on my mother's face was disgust and embarrassment. In my ten-year-old scratchy voice, I kept saying, "Mama, it's true." She just expressed that this beast said I was lying. The stare that left her eyes as she looked at this burden she had to clothe and feed. I was asking my mother for her protection. To be shunned in disbelief, to hear your mother call you a liar. But worst of all, to keep it a secret. At that moment, I knew our lives would never be the same. The beast now had my mother's love; her cup of love was empty when it came to me. I saw the hurt in my sister's eyes. She knew I was telling the truth. She just could not help. She was still young herself. She had no answers for me, and I had nothing more to say. CPS did not exist in my time.

As time passed, my mother sent me to stay with Ms. Re-Re, which meant more abuse. The monster told her I lied so she would make me stay alone in the room, away from everyone, saying I might accuse someone of rape. I cried for what seemed like ages. I just remembered my sister would come to visit me. She would sleep with the brother of this terrible woman so she could be there with me sometimes. I would cry when it was time for her to go. It was hard on me; Re-Re was not shy on punishment. A beating could come if I angered her. During this stage in my life, I began to learn about coping, pretending to be somewhere else to escape the reality that was mine to bear. So, I grew separated from my hope in God, from hope in anything other than circumstances. They were real. I know because I could feel something, even if it was pain. Now, without anyone knowing, I wanted to know who God was. Who had told me that he existed? I was ready to call them a liar. This powerful being who allows children to suffer. And so, my journey began. The lack of love had proven to be the greater gift, for the absence of love to me was a deflector of happiness.

So, I ask myself today, "What is the true definition of agape?" Thomas Aquinas explained it is "to will the good of the other." Was there no mentor for me? For many years, I held love in contempt because of my mother's betrayal. I grew confused. I could not differentiate between all forms of affection, be it predatorial or wanted. I grew up in a state of confusion. As with many missing answers to questions, I lacked guidance. That lack of guidance would steer me to a life of misguided emotions. I would become lost. I would become entwined in a life of betrayal, abuse, hate, and jealousy, but most of all, I would spend years finding my path to forgiveness. I became accustomed to unwanted gestures from men. I just created a place in my life where physical and emotional abuse were a part of the norm.

The hurt I knew was greater than any love connection I would come to encounter. Being brought up into what the world considers lower-class society would only make me cherish the crumbs that life was leaving, leading me to a trail of divided emotions. A young girl with psychotic tendencies but with the power to control and cope with the hateful thoughts that were buried deep in her subconscious. Always creating a new dream to be someone else but awakening in the same shell day in and day out. My world belonged to fate. Life became an illusion of Chicago's broken vessels. The woman I was becoming lacked a mother's love. Because of my mother's weakest moment in her dark time, I grew to convince myself to convict her, to blame her, to approve of what I had taught myself to believe about her. Weak and desperate for the love of a man. Every good thing I once loved about her was abandoned by reasoning. The day she chose him over me, she became my enemy. She was the demon I ran from, never spending much time at home. Just running, always on the move. I have now become an expert in disguises. My emotions masked, my compassion battling to exist, my grins contain so much hatred. I was turning into a beast. A beast with no control and no remorse. This is the woman those circumstances created. The Gangster Disciples had a lot of work to do with instructing me. I was very undeveloped and easily manipulated. I did not expect much from life, and I did not expect that life would come to require more from me.

Chapter One
The shadow and the Nur

The Shadows in one's thoughts are viewed as two-dimensional. Areas of darkness that conceal the light.

In the Quran, I have read that even the shadows prostrate and submit to Allah (s.w.t) (God). As I recall my walk with the GD organization, I have come to realize that it was a journey I had to take to find the Nur (light) in my life. I once was held as an inmate to the fire that I was drawn to by circumstance. Light prevailed at its appointed time, and I was no longer an inmate to my own Nafs. Freedom to choose a path after revelation was the thirst-quenching action I lacked in the past. Once I became a student in Islam, It was revealed to me that all the books come from Allah (s.w.t). This was my Path to healing. I grew up hearing my mother quote the Bible. As I embraced the truth in the Quran, I had to go back to my beginning. I knew that the Bible was based on truth. Within this truth, I had to discover my shadow and my light.

One of the greatest Chapters my mom taught to me was the 23rd Psalm. The Lord is my shepherd, and I shall not want. He maketh me to lie down in green pastures: He leadeth me beside the still waters. Remembering the scripture has helped to balance my walk in Islam. The Further reassurance from Allah (s.w.t) was me remembering psalm 91 that starts by telling," You who live in the shelter of the Most- High, who abide in the shadow of the Almighty." Allah (s.w.t) (God) had been with me this whole time. Protecting me in my days of Jahiliya (ignorance), He gives His mercy to whom he chooses.

I had been watching men of less virtue in their jealousy of one another as they perceived themselves living in someone else's shadow. That haughtiness of their position at that time in their life ushered in a rebellion that destroys the foundation of Hope. This is the demon I pray to keep at bay within my walk-in life. I cannot compare the shadow to the light because, at different points in life, they both play a significant role in self-development. As a Muslima being a student of al Islam with no Family upbringing based on its Fundamentals. My light had to come from the shadows of my beginnings. Quran Surah 21 Al- Anbya, Ayat 105 states Surely, following the heavenly Record, we decreed in the Scriptures: "My righteous servants shall inherit the land," The Zabur, as I learned it according to Islam, was the holy book of David. The Zabur that is mentioned in the Quran is the Psalms of David. One of the Holy books revealed before Islam. My mother had discovered her Path to redemption at a time my heart was bruised and closed off from accepting or allowing the teachings of Allah (s.w.t) {God} to guide me to a straighter path. I was now discovering my truth and separating this knowledge from the trickery of the loudness of the world.

The Gangster Disciples had been in the shadows of the world for years. We all came from various places in our lives trying to understand and live our truths and up to the purpose that Allah (s.w.t) had intended for us to achieve as a nation of people. In these groups of people, I believe we meet other brethren along our Path. Each with their own truth. Each with the ability to unite the masses in their ethnic background. No matter what organizational structure we have come from, Islam has united us. It's not how a path starts; it's how it ends. Whether it started with Larry Hoover, Jeff Fort, Shorty Freeman, David Barksdale, the Black Panther Party, High Supreme gangsters, etc. God has the power to change the narrative when we change what is in our hearts. Some of my shadows came from trenches on East End. We grew bonds with each other based on the truth as we knew it in our stage of Jahiliya (ignorance).

We fellowshipped together, we shared our pain, and our goal was to become financially stable in a positive manner. We had a vision full of light. The blueprint kept teaching us about similar teachings that I discover every day in my walk-in Islam as the psalms said. Thy rod and thy staff comfort me. Allah (s.w.t) (God) was there all through my state of Jahiliyah (state of ignorance). The guidance that I had received was a fragment of someone's interpretation of the dream the board members had for a group of people who were deprived of the opportunity to thrive in life. We were supposed to create our own way. Our own jobs and support the universal learning and teachings that our offspring would receive. This would have been our advantage to offset years of sacrifices that our ancestors before us had fought for. Segregation was still embedded in the hearts of many, even if the world assumed it was moving towards change. To accept the part, I played in the direction my life was steered to is to open my heart to accept forgiveness. The demon that also ravishes my thoughts is not fully releasing the hurt and the guilt. This has been the constant battle between the understanding of my shahada (declaration of Faith)

Shahada (Arabic As-Sahada) The declaration of faith, Belief in One God (Allah) and his messenger. It is one of the most sacred statements in Islam and one of the most powerful actions mankind will ever take. It is the strictness and the willingness to be able to submit one's will to Allah (God). I had learned about commitment and sacrifice within the GD organization, and it wore many faces. As the purity of Islam filtrated through my soul and resonated with my heart, the virtues of the way I chose to live my life changed. I am still always reaching back to my beginnings, as it is my duty to share my truth. My beginnings allow me to understand that individuals may travel a different route but end up in the same destination as it may be the Decree and will of Allah (s.w.t). The shadow of the voice of Larry Hoover covered me and saved me from a path of destruction in many occurrences that I had faced in life. Allah (s.w.t) can use any vessel he chooses to usher in messages and change. Study wisdom as it ought to be studied. Learn the lessons that were given and use the lessons as steppingstones to what should and should not prevail when trying to uplift a nation of people.

Allah (s.w.t) guides who He wills to the straight Path. My bother Ayyub text me, and he said Have tawakkul (trust) in Allah (s.w.t)

"I place my trust in Allah, My Lord and your Lord! There is not a moving creature, but He has a grasp of its forelock. Verily, it is my Lord that is on a straight Path (Qur 'an 11:56)

So, if we believe that there is not one creature that Allah (s.w.t) has not taken by the forelock, then I must believe in the Mercy of Allah (s.w.t). There is no creature that is not inevitably on a path that His Lord has allowed. All Paths come from Allah (s.w.t) (God), so all paths lead back to him whether man is in awe or not. So, I pray for the Mercy of Allah (s.w.t) to all my brethren. One. The one We ask ourselves the million-dollar question. Is Larry Hoover Muslim? I do not know the answers. But I do consider him as a brother and an auliyah (friend and protector). He was that to me when the shadows of my past were so overbearing, and I needed to be protected by the shadows of someone greater than men I Knew in my walk about in the Dunya.

Larry Hoover will forever be an example in my life. The Good, the mistakes, the forgiveness and the guidance have all fashioned the perseverance for change, the way I was able to open to Islam. Is man ever without fault? We all know that the answer is No. Our mistakes in the lower parts of our life lift us up to become teachers of the repercussions from choices made in error or in perceived clear judgment. The wisdom we gain can change old concepts and strengthen new ones.

(Foundation is the structure of life. Within the foundation, Hope is Elevated.) That is why Pillars exist. Pillars of light and darkness support and validate each other. In Islam, the Five Pillars are our Core Beliefs and practices. The shahada (The belief that "There is no god but God, and Muhammad is the Messenger of God",

Prayer (salat) I have witnessed the universal power of the salat with brothers and sisters I once would not have imagined bowing and prostrating together.

Alms (zakat) In days of ignorance, man seemed to be for himself. I am witnessing the power to think beyond one's selfishness. Whether it be financial, a smile, sharing your labor, knowledge or a meal. Putting the care of others for the sake of Allah (s.w.t) (God) above all else.

Fasting (sawm) The Holy Month of Ramadan. Or on a Tuesday and Thursday. A pillar of an intent to strengthen one's Deen and relationship with the creator.

Pilgrimage (hajj) The once in a lifetime journey to Mecca for those who are able. These are the Muslim Creed.

There was a time when We, as a group of people, pledged our love, life and our loyalty and embraced in teachings of an Honorable chairman. Having understood that fundamental concept. We were being guided and prepared for the ushering in of light once we had taken our shahada (declaration of Faith).

In every structure and foundation, spirituality must be present. Spirituality is the light that balances the thoughts and decisions that govern the way one lives.

As a Muslima, I now know that had I received the revelation sooner than the appointed time it was revealed, my foundation may not have been as solid as it is today. Even with my imperfections, I believe in the constancy of turning to my Guardian lord in tawba (the act of asking Allah (s.w.t.) for forgiveness, repenting from the sins that I have made). This is what brings me closer to Allah (s.w.t.) (God). Shadows and light will always surround our being.

Chapter Two

Prejudice

Prejudice had been given a description, in my opinion, growing up. Islam is the purity and the shield that transforms confusion and chaos into quiet and calm. I had understood racism based on my experience as an African American young woman. It appeared to just be the differences between Caucasian and African American views. I would come to learn that my whole being was surrounded by racism. As a former member of a street organization, I held prejudices against other organizations as we perceived ourselves to be better than others. This was indeed prejudice. Each organization had come from Strong leaders, Mr. Larry Hoover, Mr. Jeff Fort, Mr. David Barksdale, Mr. Willie Lloyd, etc. We each needed financial stability, we each had our own ideologies and our way of life. But we each somehow saw each other's way of life to be lower than the standards we were practicing.

This is indeed prejudice. When I, Mel, Nine and Sharon were hanging out on East End on the Esat side of Chicago. All we could see was the vision we believed we were representing through our actions. Actions I now believe can cause a ripple effect on society. We were entrusted to be an example of Growth and Development. We fellowshipped and trusted in each other. But we never trusted in each other enough to call each other out on our imperfections. We were young. We were hungry for the ideology of Growth and Development, but we had not conditioned our minds to understand what that fully entailed. As good brothers in the organization, they were to me and Sharon. We were safe, and they were there if we needed Aid and assistance.

But in all that loyalty, I realized now that I had a prejudice and a fear. I was very cautious of what I called back then oppositions. Without that spiritual foundation, we lived in a world of separation. Today, I witnessed my Muslim brother Mustafa, formerly known as Prince Wakeeta, pray and hold fast to the rope of Allah (s.w.t) (God). The same rope of Allah (s.w.t) (God) that I am trying every day to hold on to. Islam is the teaching in life that has allowed me to release the shackle from my feet. Prejudice is the destroyer of life and Hope. Holding on to it can sabotage the strength of a nation. Blindfold the believing men and women who fight for so much change. Prejudice can create a dangerous surrounding when it goes undetected.

I had to study it. Racism lies within our present and our past. Even in Biblical scripture, racism existed amongst the tribes. All through religious scripture, it is present. I pray to gain the knowledge to uplift all mankind no matter what walk we have come from. The scriptures that were not revealed in my younger years say

"O you who believe! Let not a group mock at another group,

it may be the latter are better than the former: Nor let (some) women mock at other women; it may be that the latter are better than the former, nor defame one another, Nor insult one another by nicknames. How bad is it to insult one's brother after having faith. And whosoever does not repent, then such are indeed the wrongdoers "(Chapter 49)

I must support Justice. Steer from bias. I must extend the patience and the kindnesses my Lord has

Given to me. I served well as a Sister of the struggle. Now, I must serv well as a student of Islam. To remember when I once knew not. So, let there be no confusion from my walk-in life. I identify as a Muslim sister. I Still care about brothers and sisters of the struggle. I most definitely care about all the former leaders that are incarcerated and being held. They are people. A part of creation. A part of creation that I know personally or have studied their walk-in life. I pray that the Mercy of Allah (s.w.t) touches their lives. What mercy looks like, I do not know. Allah (s.w.t) (God) know what I know not.

I do know that to release prejudice is to open on all levels. To search for the understanding to grow and develop as was intended for me so many years ago. Finding my purpose in life despite the hurt and the betrayal that life offered me as a young girl. It was my test and my trial. Today, I chose to see the best of the people I once fellowshipped with. To see the best in the people I once did not understand. To see brother Jaleel, whom I once knew as Thel, to see Prince Wakeeta, who is now known as brother Mustafa, so humbled by Allah (s.w.t). (God) has a power so deep within my understanding that surpasses everything I once believed. My Muslim Brothers and sisters from the West side of Chicago. K town. Rooster, who is now brother Kareem, white Boy, who is now Brother Sabir. This is a blessing to see you in the Nur (light) of this world. This world has tested us all.

We have survived with a purpose by the will of Allah (s.w.t). We are still a mirror for each other. We still want for our brothers and sisters what we want for ourselves. Alhamdulillah, to see Prince Wakeeta, now Brother Mustafa, Thel, now known as Brother Jaleel, Tyree, who is now Muslim, and White Boy, who is brother Sabr. Just so many Muslims that the fragrance of my tears of joy for seeing the power of Allah (s.w.t) in what I call my miracle. Is like being awakened after a long slumber in life. We lost a lot of good people to the Penal system. That system destroyed many relationships. It was treacherous. It forced groups of people to choose. That is a hard pill to swallow. When I was incarcerated, I saw many families feuding because they had to make a choice. My love and understanding goes out to those who had to choose.

My love and, understanding, and prayers go out to those who decided to stand firm on their beliefs. We were all trapped by the shackle's society placed on us as an organization. Shorty G, Jimmy D, Lil Frank, Big A, Lil Dave etc. My compassion will always supersede man's logic. We once considered ourselves Larry's finest. Astaghfirallah (May Allah (s.w.t) Forgive), we still tease each other sometimes in conversation as we express a time in our life when all we knew was each other. Just as the Penal group brings brothers and sisters together, the walks in our spirituality seal the balance in those relationships we formed. I now know what universal love is. I did not comprehend it at first. I can now identify it. I saw it in prison when I hit the grounds in Alderson, west Virginia. My Muslim sisters came with shoes and clothing to make sure I was okay. Then I saw it again in Danbury, Connecticut. I was learning the love that Islam places between believers. Prejudice had to take the backseat. Islam, Love Mercy sat in the front.

Chapter Three

The Bond

Long before my journey started, bonds were formed. Lives were developing and growing. The world had not tapped into this perception. In 1969, two years before my birth, a bond formed between the late David Barksdale and Larry Hoover. The unification of two African American men who showed us an example of a bond. United to become the BGDN nation. This is what Wikipedia has to say. These two men have played a significant part of the information I learned growing up as a young teenager. The information they have passed down through half of the Century has allowed many of us to know what a bond is. The scaredness of a bond, the brokenness when a bond has stopped living up to its promise or its full potential. Where my Path crossed could not be blamed on a bond. I hear the world, and some people take aim and blame men of color to drown out the corruption of this world. Bonds have always been formed to unite a group of individuals to accomplish a goal. Bonds for the greater Good.

During these bonds, many may not factor in the powerful effect that circumstances play in the outcome of the things hoped for. I wanted to bring peace and uplift the voices of women. This is how my bond formed with the GD organization. The bond was solid as far as I am concerned. I just lacked the fundamental tools to cultivate that bond in my younger years. Lack of financial knowledge, lack of a solid spiritual background and a lack of understanding of what a bond really means. So much time has been lost because of the lack of knowledge, because of broken trust and the abandonment of loyalty. We can blame our failures on as many people as we like. Ultimately, we know deep down inside the sources of our failures, for so many, are Greed, Power, money, pride and prejudice. The mere things that spirituality warns against. Balancing spiritual enlightenment within the bonds that formed over the years is a great mystery. It's very complicated to hold it altogether along with your walk with Allah (s.w.t) (God). You are constantly trying not to commit a Shirk (there are three types of Shirk: The Major shirks (Ash-Shirk 2. Minor shirks Ash-Shirk al As-ghar and 3 the inconspicuous Shirk Ash-Shirk al-Khafi).

Examples of Shirk in Islam are showing off, abandoning prayer, swearing by Allah (s.w.t), loving others more than Allah (s.w.t), believing in Bad omens, fearing others more than Allah (s.w.t), seeking help from others more than Allah (s.w.t). The greatest shirk is setting someone up with Allah (s.w.t), a rival, and He is the one that created you. So, by upholding a bond with someone, I must try and make sure that I follow the constraints of my religious beliefs. I will forever have a Love for Mr. Hoover. He has fashioned how I am able to perceive the revelation from Allah (s.w.t.). He did this by allowing me to learn and fear rules that governed us when I was a member of the GD organization. He introduced me to my silver before I had been granted my Gold. (Islamic teachings.) Now, in Islam, I have a bond with my brethren and Sisters in Islam. I want for them what I want for myself. This stomps out the greed that many conceal in their hearts. I have always been contenting in life with my finances. Always grateful to just be among the people I fellowshipped with. Never having a Love for money. It came and went. I am grateful that I have always been this way. Greed was never my enemy, I never welcomed it as a friend.

However, putting men and women on pedestals was. I now can have respect for their position in life without associating that respect with any upliftment higher than my creator. I study the wisdom they possess and carry. I listen to the words they speak out of mutual respect. I take from it what lines up with scripture, and I leave that alone, which I have no understanding for. With all the hurt I have endured from my family, Islam was clear. Never break the bond of Kinship. Even though my heart has ached during my walk-in life. I must Uphold the ties of Kinship. This means kind treatment of relatives according to the position of each of them. This was hard. But this is Islam.

Abdullah ibn 'Amr ibn al-As (pbuh) reported that the Prophet (pbuh) said: "The one who upholds ties of kinship is not the one who recompenses the good done to him by his relatives: rather, he is the one who keeps good relations with those relatives who had severed the bond of kinship with him."

I was angry when my daughter passed. Angry at what had been allowed from a Decree of Allah (s.w.t.). I went about pointing fingers at what should have been done on what wasn't done. I missed the fact that all the family loved my beautiful Star in their own way. It was not my place to question what Allah (s.w.t) did not prevent. Everything good comes from Allah (s.w.t) (God). I just needed to find peace with that in my spirit. Forgiveness is a bond that I must plant inside my spirit, my mind and my heart. Cherishing the bond that Allah (s.w.t) let me experience in my daughter's short walk on this earth. I had already allowed in my younger years a bond to be ravaged between me and my mom with hate and confusion. That generational gap must stop somewhere. It stops here today, now.

My stepmom Roberta had a bond so strong with my dad, Willie Hobson. The father whose name I never carried. Her bond was so strong that she was able to love me and give me what I needed in the short time I knew her. I know that now. So, no matter how much of my money I gave her, I have no regrets now. I spoke of it because I was expressing the hurt, I needed to let go. The anger and jealousy I felt with my cousins. Her nieces. The anger I felt about the choice and the disposal of what they had worked for. Feeling at one point that I was betrayed after doing that prison sentence and protecting their property. No, I did what a loyal daughter does. Protect her family. There should never be any recompense for that. That is the bond of Kinship. In return, she has left me the love of the only thing she could offer to me. Family, Gayle, Tina, Sheena, Roberta, Ilene, Carol, Andrea. They have always held on to us even when we did not know how to hold on to ourselves. She shared her family. My family now.

She had left me the best of herself. Family bonds. Even my family in Mississippi, which I have a lot of, but my cousin Tonya. She washed me up when I got shot. Pregnant and with a cast on my arm. She was pregnant, too. We all were at the same time. Two sisters and one cousin. I could not reach to wash my private areas. I was embarrassed and full of hurt. G Sharp death had taken its toll of my life at that time. Tonya reached and washed me and reminded me that we were family. Hurt and pain can block the clouds of goodness if you let it. Star is gone, and I see the life my daughter once lived reflecting in my face. A tragedy no mother or father ever wants to endure. In this pain, I am finding the love and support that is still here. Family, Bonds, Hope and healing. Bonding with Life and with Purpose. I wanted to blame Nikki because she always let Star runway to her home. Nikki thought she was saving her. Can I be so angry that I have not acknowledged the love our offspring had for one another. Cousins. Cousins that loved each other despite their differences. As adults, we demand that children choose between their love and their bonds with people.

This is the demon one must fight. The demon to try and

control or expect the outcome of another's action. I allowed that demon in my life in ignorance, trying to protect Star from my demons. Was it the right choice, I don't know. What I do know is that she loved all her family. Even those she did not see eye to eye with at times. To remember Star is to remember the love she tried to unite between us all. Bonds are deep. They exist in everything and everywhere. Bonds are what keep relationships sacred.

I can say that because one night in particular, my brother said Lisa, they are talking about shooting up the house down there in Lucedale, MS. My Aunt Jackie and My Uncle Johnny home. Home to my late mother. After speaking with Shawn, it didn't matter who was wrong. What mattered is this was serious. My Uncle is a preacher and a good man. My aunt, his wife, means well. They just sometimes lack religious tolerance. I was worried. Then, those bonds came into play. Ted had gotten Lil Larry on the phone for me with the speed of lightning. Lil Larry said quickly. Nobody bet not touch a preacher or shoot up church. We, as having been students of the GD organization before, knew that was ridiculous. We were not sure how it happened. What we were sure of was this is not Growth and Development. It was within an hour or so if my recollection serves me right. My cousin called and said I am not sure what you did, but it's over. They said we were good. I was pissed still at my family. Respect is something that should be practiced daily in life. Somewhere, something had gotten out of hand.

But a true bond between individuals that formed in my younger years saved my family in my older years. Bonds are so significant. You can never forget where you come from. It's in your DNA. I remember the Imam said, if you went hard in those streets, I believe you will go hard in Islam. It is in your character. So, not only has Mr. Hoover touched my life as an individual. He has touched my life through the blessed relationships with his family. Both Larry Bernard and Lil Larry I have been blessed to have known in my life. Known them to be caring men in life. Supportive to communities. That comes from true guidance whether the world holds on to their prejudices. I choose to hold on to Love, Hope, mercy. Insha Allah (s.w.t), the creator, gives his kingdom to who he chooses. I am just a vessel to share a message with those I once knew. Share Islam.

Chapter Four
Trust (Amaanah)

When I began to study the word trust or its action in my life, I had to see how trust aligned with my religious beliefs. One of the things that I had read was there is no faith for one who cannot be trusted. The Surah 81 Ayat 21: "Those who faithfully observe their trusts and their covenants." Surah 23 Ayat 8 says, "Return the trust to those who entrusted you and do not betray those who betrayed you". These words were solidification that trust encompasses honesty, and it has superseded the questions challenging loyalty. It has been written that the Prophet (PBUH) often use to say, "Why don't you tie down your camel? I have to tie my camel down. This is the constant battle between what I once knew and what I have come to learn. Balancing the trust that others have placed with me. The trust that brothers and sisters have given me in my former relationships before Islam. I have researched that trust has two meanings, a general meaning and a specific meaning. The general meaning will cover my covenant to Islam. All Allah (s.w.t) commands and those things that is prohibited to me. The underlying fact is that it is a sense of responsibility and accountability.

Maybe that dictates my actions in fulfilling contracts, promises, covenants and trusts. Amaanah(trust) is something that we often look for within the individuals we come in communion with.

Before Islam, trust was complicated in the Dunya, probably because of the lack of spiritual guidance and the separation from the creator through a lack of understanding and guidance. Al-Anfaal 8:27 Verily Allah commands that you should render back the trusts to those to whom they are due. I have to live as an example of my walk in Islam. But I believe that every individual should have the truth and that light shared with them. So yes, I will always think and offer my dua's for Larry Hoover, Jeff Fort, The Board. Allah (s.w.t) Guides whom he pleases to the straight Path. It is never my choice to choose or suggest whose heart and mind he touches.

I have lately tried to surround myself with positivity. This reflects our intended teachings from the Blueprints. However, it also said trust none suspect all. Dissecting the definition of that statement for myself made me realize how much one can be a hypocrite themselves when people observe mistakes made by individuals connected to their group. I wonder if they ever observe their own mistakes. Probably not. In Islam, Backbiting is frowned upon. The Bible also speaks of slander. So, when I look over my life, I see that some of my actions in my state of Jahiliyah (ignorance) may have caused confusion. To accept the humanness of man is to be able to forgive oneself. To deny that some actions of man may not have been intentional or was unintentional is to exhibit the characteristics of a hypocrite. I cannot tear open a man or woman heart and see what is in it. I can only express Allah (s.w.t) Mercy and His word that if my servant walks to me in repentance, then I am swift to run to him.

I must trust in Allah (s.w.t) (God) and pray that I make positive choices about the company I keep. So, I was grateful that a person who had spent such little time around me cared enough to question if I was okay in my return to the city. Those with genuine concern for my mind, body and soul. Being in the city at times has its flashbacks. The mind cannot erase the sound of continuous gunshots that threatened your life. I Have come to know that Allah (s.w.t) is a protector and as long as I hold fast to the rope of Allah (s.w.t). My destiny is in Allah (s.w.t) hands.

Further, I came across the question of why we Love all, respect a few and trust no one. I think we have expectations of people, of groups. When our expectations are not met, we assume they failed us. Maybe we failed ourselves by putting too much on an individual. Not trusting that he or she did their best with what they were given. I was so wrapped up in the mistakes that G Sharp had made concerning me that I forgot about the goodness that he shared. I will never condone Physical or mental abuse. I like to accept the power of its healing. The power to take control and rebuild. Forgiveness is so much sweeter than constantly reliving trauma. I am now in control of my actions, although Allah (s.w.t) (God) is in control of the seasons in my life. My Qadr (destiny).

As brother Ayyub constantly supports my willingness to share the changes in our lives as we reverted from our old beliefs to Islam, He has shared with me the brotherhood and sisterhood in spaces he has been and traveled. I felt blessed and comfortable as the prayer was being offered Jumah Friday on 39. th. I was not in salat this day. As I observed and heard the Adhan (Muslim call to prayer), the power of the words I heard and the prayers I observed uplifted my spirit. The trust that those Muslim Brothers and sisters were protectors and it filled the air. Brother Abdul (Jalil/Baahir imports) was so kind every time we crossed paths. Pure love and respect solely for the sake of Allah (s.w.t). I was just in constant awe because twenty years ago, I was praying to be in the midst of Muslims in the free world. Today was a reminder of Allah (s.w.t) (God's) mercy and His promise as he has dominion over my life.

Later that day, I would be surrounded by Muslims again in a park near to my past. My mother had a house on 79th in Loomis, and we would not dare go to Foster Park, which was just blocks away in my younger years... In my day, the twins Rino and Dino, as they were called, did not have no GDs in that territory. Today, I was witnessing the Power of God to change and heal the disease in the heart of man. Brother Mustafa (aka Prince Wakeeta) was there praying. They were going to different areas each week to offer salat. I know I am to lower my gaze as a Muslima in Islam. However, my eyes were fixated because I never dreamed this possible before

Islam. I now see how our Leaders and teachers could fathom the ability for peace. We were just missing Islam.

This means that there was some kind of love or inclination of Good within these brothers all the time. They just had not completely tapped into the Power of Allah (s.w.t) (God) whole heartedly with the knowledge they possess today. They were all on their journey. All would somehow play a major part in my walk-in life. Some as teachers, some as those reminders of Allah (s.w.t) mercy and love for his creation, some as protectors, but more significantly. Many are now my brothers and sisters in Islam. I caution those to remember when we knew not. We share the Dawah as is our responsibility. I do not speak on who should get the mercies from Allah (s.w.t). That I have no proof of. If a prostitute at a well lowered her shoe and gave an animal drinking water, and she got forgiveness for that mere action. Who am I to question who Allah (s.w.t) will give His mercy too. It is my duty to keep sharing the light that is shining so bright in my time of healing. As Muslims, yes, we fellowship together and associate no partners with Allah (s.w.t), but he has also mentioned the Children of the book so many times that I pass no judgement. Just forgiveness and understanding where I believe that I have been wronged. I beg forgiveness in places that I may have erred. This is the trust (the Tawakkul) that I have in Allah (s.w.t).

Bismillah

As the day ushers in the Dhur and I hear the voices of my brethren praying at this moment in my life, my spirit has embraced its truth and blocked out the remnants of today's strife.

We are in the care of the creator, bound one to another. It is here in Islam where I have found trust is my sister and my brother.

As the Asr prayers sets in and, I am surrounded by brothers and sisters. This is where a new journey begins.

My eyes stare into the wonders of Allah (s.w.t) Universe how the creator instills the power to love and change the generational curse. We are as one in Islam.

I can see the power and strength of nations of people who have transformed to enhance a larger nation of men and women. A nation of People. A nation of Muslims. A nation practicing Al Islam.

Foster Park was now illuminating that which I had never done to the finest of victories, I was there, and prayers were being offered as one.

This is the Power of Allah (s.w.t) (God).

Amana "trust, honesty, responsibility and integrity in all the duties which Allah (s.w.t) has placed upon humans. This comes from the Muslim community and education.

It has enlightened me of my responsibility to all my covenant and my trust to the believing Men and women. As Believers, we beseech Allah (s.w.t) (God) to guide us all in walks of life in, which is absolutely true. I have witnessed the line straight and tight and could feel the power of the strength of unity my brethren were exemplifying into the Universe. It was not in the Middle East; it was right here on the south side of Chicago. It was my truth being reminded that I have to have faith that Allah (s.w.t) is my protector. Who am I to not relinquish all my trust in the virtues that He has instilled into his creation. Allah (s.w.t) guides who he wills to the Sirat ul Mustaqim (straight Path.) The trustworthiness of my brothers and sisters supersedes what I had learned and witnessed in the Dunya.

Allah (s.w.t) the Highest has said, "But if one of you trusts another, then he who is trusted should deliver his trust, and let him be careful (of his duty to Allah (s.w.t) (God.) Never have I, in such a long time, felt so much peace and reassurance of Allah (s.w.t) mercy as I have felt on my journey as I have begun to write. To share, to accept the Gold I have been given. Islam. Many of my brethren and sisters have parallel paths that has guided us to Islam. Despite the Path, I took to Islam. If I had to trust my brothers and sisters in Islam. The answer is yes. No matter what I have been a part of. My trust is in every word that has been written for guidance. Therefore, at this time in my life, it is necessary that every Muslim should be Ameen (trustworthy) In the Shariah, Trust has abroad sense. Betrayal of trust is a sin, a major sin. So, I have to be vigilant and practice that which I beseech from my Muslim brothers and sisters. The rights that I have over them, the rights that they have over me.

For the curious, those rights are when to give other Muslims when you meet them the greeting of peace. When invited, you are to respond to the invitation, when a Muslim seeks your advice, advise. When a Muslim sneezes and praises Allah (s.w.t) (God), supplicate for mercy for them. When he becomes ill, visit him. When they die, follow them (their funeral). This is the Decree. This is the Path of those who fear Allah (s.w.t).

So, Thank you, Black. Know you are appreciated in this journey as we share our truth, Our triumphs and our mistakes. Failure is not an option. We just keep striving to do better. Masha Allah.

Chapter Five

The Qadr (Decree of Allah (s.w.t))

Years I have spent wondering why my Path in life was so bumpy. I asked many times why my parents were not Muslim. The Imam had explained that if my revelation befell me sooner. I might not be a student of Islam. I was still very indecisive about the answer. However, facts were I came from a background of Christianity, and I was not able to comprehend it until later on in life. All the studies from the Bible academy only allowed me to perceive the power of the unexplainable. Growing up, I was told to walk by faith and not by sight. It's my opinion that you need them both. So many soldiers have fought for what they believed in. One of the noblest things a man or woman can do. Imagine learning that you had faith in hypocrisy too late to change the outcome of your action as it sits in its present state. You can witness your brother steal money, backbite, slander, murder, rape, lie. Your sight sees and acknowledges this to be true. Yet you have faith in their ability to lead you to a different path. This is where I challenge the hypocrisy in myself. I don't expect man to guide me anywhere. He shares, enlightens and solidifies the truth of his actions.

I pray for Allah (s.w.t) to guide me to the truth because our minds cannot fully phantom Allah's purpose. He uses many vessels to show the evidence of his mercy. I learned the parable of the story of the man who killed 99 people. A well-known parable in Islam that teaches the importance of repentance and forgiveness. According to a hadith in Sahih Muslim, the Prophet (PBUH) told us about a man who killed 99 people. This man asked who the most knowledgeable person in the land and was directed to a monk. After he was informed about the man's crimes, the monk told him he cannot repent for murdering 99 people. The man killed him, which meant he had now killed 100 people. He asked again about the most knowledgeable man person in the land and was told about a scholar. After going to him, he asked the scholar if he could repent for the 100 murders. The scholar said that he certainly can, asking him who could prevent him from doing so. He instructed him to go to a certain land where people worship Allah and join them in worshipping him. He also told him not to return to his land, as it was a bad land. The man who killed 99 people then headed for the land the scholar had told him about. When he had completed half of his journey, he passed away. The angels of mercy and the angels of punishment proceeded to dispute over his fate. The angels of mercy pointed out his repentance and the fact that he was turning to Allah in sincerity.

On the other hand, the angels of punishment remarked that he didn't do any good in his life. An angel then came in human form, and they allowed him to mediate. He instructed them to measure the distance between his destination and the land he came from, saying that he belongs to the land that he is closer to. Upon measuring the distance, they discovered that he was closer to the land he was going to, so the angels of mercy took him.

I reverted back to this Hadith because in my walk and, many of the brothers and sisters reading my books are all wondering how I have felt so partial to those who the world may perceive as lost or not worthy of the Mercy of Allah (s.w.t). I don't want to get caught up in the stigma of this world. It is not my place to do so. What I do know is a person can come an arm's length of the hell fire and make it to heaven (Jannah), as Jannah (heaven being one of the six articles of faith in Islam. We all strive for it. So yes, I have mercy on any individual caught up in the repercussions of the Dunya. For me, I say some names because those names surrounded me my whole life. These names Larry Hoover, Jeff Fort, Prince Wakeeta before he was Mustafa, that is how I can study the word of God. I am witnessing his mercy as I watch the world directly around me. The same way I study the time that came before me.

I am not placing great emphasis on an individual's journey; I am praying for the final destination. This is why I try to leave the three most significant things behind after my departure, an ongoing charity, beneficial knowledge, or a righteous child who prays for me after my crossing to another realm. For Muslims this endeavor, this action is very well known. For those People of the book and anyone else who identifies with something different, I will expound on the knowledge that I have gained.

According to the Hadith on Sahih Bukhari, the Prophet (pbuh) said that when a person dies, their deeds come to an end except for three things: ongoing charity, beneficial knowledge, or a righteous child who prays for them.

Ongoing Charity refers to any charitable act, digging a well, donating to a charitable organization a school that teaches the word of God. In can come in many forms, but it is one of the three things the keep going on after you leave this realm.

Knowledge that will benefit another. Religious knowledge, scientific knowledge, or any knowledge that will benefit creation.

A righteous child that prays for their parents after death. The child's prayers are believed to benefit in the afterlife.

So, no matter how much I speak about my past, I pray that you hold tight to every word that Allah (s.w.t.) has allowed you to be enlightened by. I do not make excuses for my mistakes or others that I have known. I share the power of healing. Many great men and women have come from paths parallel to where they would have wanted to start in life. Allah (s.w.t) knew you and what you would encounter. He understood the essence of your nature. He gave us free will and free choice for this free will, and free choice is your test from God. In Islam Qadr (predestination or divine destiny), I know not why my life crossed paths with so many individuals from all walks in life and organizational structures. I can only trust in

Allah (s.w.t) to guide my understanding.

Another parable related to my conversation on my Qadr (divine revelation) is the story of Prophet Musa (Moses) and (Khidr). In this story, Musa (pbuh) meets Khidir, who is believed to be a prophet or a saint. Khidr performs several actions that seem unjust or inexplicable to Prophet Musa (pbuh). However, Khidir explains that these actions were a part of God's plan and was necessary for a greater good. This story teaches us that we may not always understand Allah's plan and that they were necessary for the greater Good. This story teaches us that we may not always understand God's plan, but we should trust in His wisdom and accept His decisions. May Allah (s.w.t) have mercy on me if I have not expressed myself as clearly as I should. I am not a scholar. I am a student of Islam.

Fighting against many vices in this modern-day walk. So, it is my desire to open up this walk to study it so that others who are struggling in the same area can study their circumstances for themselves. Each one teaches one. Yes, I must deviate and turn from the ways of my past. I have to pray for continuous guidance to try and stay on the Path that leads away from the hell fire. This is done through constant repentance. Trying to sincerely create change in this world and be as transparent as I can as well as forgiving as I can. I would in a heartbeat trust any Muslim Striving for the straightway no matter what walk in life they came from.

In Islam, trust is a great component to a brotherhood or sisterhood. Muslims are encouraged to trust and support one another, especially in times of need. The Quran states that "the believers are but brothers, so make settlement between your brothers. And fear Allah that you may receive mercy."

Trust (Amana) is also greatly emphasized in the hadiths of the Prophet (pbuh). For example, he said that "a Muslim is the brother of another Muslim. He does not wrong him, nor does he abandon him when he is in need". This Hadith highlights the importance of helping and supporting each other in difficult times. I also realize that trust should not be blind or unconditional. Muslims are to verify information and to be cautious when dealing with others. The Prophet (pbuh) said that" it is enough of a lie for a man to speak everything he hears." This teaches us to be careful about what we say and verify before spreading it.

Amana (trust) is an important aspect in the Islamic brotherhood and sisterhood in Islam.

Allah (s.w.t) knows what choices humans will make because He has predetermined everything that will happen in the world…. This means that humans are responsible for their actions and will be held accountable for it on the day of recompense (judgment). It is not for me to pass the judgement. It is my duty to share the love and, knowledge, and wisdom that has befallen me over the years. This land cannot heal its diseases until it discovers where it all originated from.

Insha Allah, I hope this helps.

Chapter Six

The Wahi (Guidance from the Creator /Revelation/intervention)

When I was incarcerated, many revelations came to past. I would say I encountered a reckoning with my own intervention. The first year was definitely my hardest. I was carrying life in my womb. I was going away for an extremely long period of time. During the silence and the quietness, I could hear all the voices that had been tuned out over time. This is when I understood the power of back-biting and gossiping and the destruction it entails, even in the truth. Shocking revelations about your life and the state of disarray you left it in could be an extremely unpleasant surprise. In the English dictionary, Wahi means to make known to reveal.

In Islam, it is known as Wahee (Arabic word for revelation), also spelled Wahy or Wahyu. As I took my Shada, I began to discover many forms of revelations that were designed for my development. The preparation to usher in the season of tests and trials. Many of those tests were the separation of relationships I would come in contact with. The Federal system will ship you all over the United States to be housed. You are bound to meet people who share past interests or bonds to a particular subject or group of individuals. I met an old friend from Peoria whom I did state time with and two cousins that I would never have met under any other circumstance. This is how distant my family bloodline is. I came across Sisters of the Struggle from Peoria, Chicago, and also a young lady from the coast of Mississippi. We were all housed in Texas during my first year as a student of Islam. This year would prove to be a very difficult year. I fell in a couple of different categories of social groups.

Family that I had not met before, but you can call out to discover that they were indeed cousins. One from my grandmother's side and one from my grandfather's side. Then there were past street ties. Trying to identify with each group was very challenging. The Sisters of the Struggle were on the compound, and we were fellowshipping as one would do so far away from home. Then salat would come in, and the Muslim sisters, who were very patient, would simply remind me that It's not what I am doing at this time that I should be mindful of. They reminded me to be conscious that prayer time was in. They would reveal to me how I exercise my right to pray on the prison jobs and took full advantage of that right, but then in socializing, I would put the salat off a little longer in my conversations with peers. This is what we identify with as a common bid'ah in Islam. (Bid'ah meaning an innovation) In Islam, we believe that every innovation leads to the hell fire.

In my discovery, it was not that I socialized with people I understood. It was based on the fact that my worship in Islam also revolved around prayer (salat). Which was taking precedent over my actions and my religious beliefs. I compare this revelation because many of my brothers and sisters also struggle with the same balance. In our relationships with our former lives or even our current situations will come a time where you will have to choose between an action to try and keep yourself grounded. There are two types of bid'ah that I was introduced to too. Bid'ah hasanah good innovation) and Bida Sayyiah Bad innovation. I still, in my present day, find this a struggle. I share this with any religious group because Allah (s.w.t) time is His and His alone. His divinity is His and His alone. I have spent a constant battle with time. Time is the Creators handy work. Allah and his command throughout history has dictated our understandings, accomplishments and our shortcomings. The creator is Eternal, so time does not encompass Him as it does man. So, I pray to be mindful that I am only on this plane for a limited time, and I try to monitor my actions and behaviors to the best of my ability, as all believing men and women should.

The question is sharing the Dawah, which means to enlighten. Giving Dawah to me when I was incarcerated did not always show immediate results, but it was my responsibility to share it. I try not to become so consumed that I disrespect the individual that I must share it with. So, my relationships with groups of people I pray to always continue, just be very mindful of the dangers it can have on my religious beliefs. I am not so concerned about the way the world views me. I am more concerned about my heart and what it contains. This is why I do not Shun any person or group. Many of the brothers and sisters that are incarcerated have so much mental stigma to deal with that I have vowed not to be a handicap to others. When I was fighting for my freedom, the district attorney said that I was a menace to society and was against my freedom. He could only see what lay between the lines and paragraphs that a group of people hurried to put together. This is not to say I had not erred in life. It is just to say that the courts could have no true knowledge of how my future was going to unravel after my release.

There is one thing that I must agree with, is that we need laws and discipline sometimes as reminders to help balance our walk within our own truths. Within these laws has to be spirituality, and one has to establish one's own relationship with Allah (s.w.t). I often listen to many Podcasts, just praying that I can understand and get a feel for others opinions because they sometimes differ from mine. As a humanitarian, I like to extract the mistakes and misunderstandings made by people to try to encourage change. One can never hold on to a person at his weakest state in their time of Jahiliyah. When we pass those judgments, we are asking ourselves to be judged by the same measure. My Emaan (belief and faith) fluctuates. I have always had highs and lows since I was old enough to feel hurt, pain and love. Sometimes, my disobedience causes shackles and in prisons me with my desires (shahwa). Theres not a captive or a soul imprisoned by his own desires that is free unless that soul learns to conquer their desires. Out of all the prisons I have feared in my limitless time on earth. I fear the whim of my desires. I have found it hard to move forward when I am constantly being attacked by circumstances that cause me to act upon my desires, whether in a low state or an elevated one.

As I accept my truths for myself, I must have mercy on my brothers and sisters who are facing the same demon. Hawa (desire). An individual who is trapped by confusion will defend themselves. Many desires may come in to play, causing injury to the world around them. So, as I fight for the understanding of Influential men and women who need the mercy of understanding, I have to also fight for levels of understanding of the dangers of my desires, be they good or unintentional, against my religious beliefs. When I am at my stronger plane spiritually and mentally, I ascend higher from the reaches of my desires. It is when my fight for balance loses its grip that I can descend to lower places within my heart. This will always be a test and a trial for many. Many of those around me may not even know that we have the same fight. We view our walk in many different ways. I pray that my Taqwa (God consciousness) keeps me from fearing my position to give the Dawah and Mercy to all even when it is not a popular opinion of people. I want my works to edify the power of forgiveness and the mercy that the creator gives to His Creation. Not to be confused with my past as a sister of the struggle. Each has its own grip upon the elevation in the direction my Path is traveling. Let those who have ears to hear, hear my truth. Let there be no compulsion in religion. I understand that truth stands clear from error. I just pray to understand does that mean we stop fighting for the mercy of those who the world has forgotten.

Chapter Seven

Beauty

I WAS BEAUTIFUL ONCE upon a time in a land where little girls play.

My heart would feel the melodies from the chirps of the birds in the morning when little girls awake to pray.

My eyes were once beautiful. I could see color through the storm clouds that hovered above. Rays of sunshine would burst through the haze of gray on most rainy days.

Beauty was within my soul, not among the flesh of man. Beauty once could whisper that this God I used to call on had the entire world in his hand.

I was once beautiful before I met the beast that lurks inside of man.

Chapter Eight

Violence

GROWING UP SO fast leads to childish decisions assumed to be correct from a young girl's perspective. One of these decisions would bring down the wrath of man. Or, as one would say today, the wrath of a complete coward. When a man strikes a woman instead of his intended target, he is the worst kind of coward. An abuser, a man who can find his only match from the feminine side of the universe.

A true man teaches with his speech. He feeds his woman's soul with assurance that he is a protector, and his concerns are her care spiritually and mentally. He relishes the fact that she has been fashioned from the rib and created to be a helpmate and not a servant. He explains his dislikes and concerns, leaving his significant other with room to process and taste his feelings; in return, she can digest the hunger of his disappointment.

In that breathtaking moment, she can evaluate the misbehavior, if any, on her behalf. This constitutes communication from both parties. Understanding then becomes mutual.

Within my outrage with life, I met the total opposite man. My black eye stemmed from his weakness to confront the real threats he had. He was a part of this sect of guys who decided to branch out on their own from the brothers of the struggle to become the crew once known as the Boggish Boys, a newly created sect that the Gangster Disciples were not fond of. This man I had chosen to love in my chaotic way once held my respect. When I knew him, he had so much control over other individuals that it fascinated me. In my ignorance of the streets, I had put this coward on a pedestal that was only ever designed for the creator of creations. God. I was just running from the master.

As I observed what was going on, I realized all the money he flashed before my eyes belonged to someone else. He was on the front, as they say in the dope game. A front he mishandled. A front that would open my eyes for many years to come. I learned he was short by a few thousand. To a seventeen-year-old runaway from home, his world seemed spectacular, his world of fraud. As they took his car and beat his ass, he came in and beat mine. Upon his arrival, I only asked how his day was. Then his fist rang out in the air; as I ran away, all I could hear were gunshots. This weak-ass coward was shooting at me. Like I hurt him. Later, as I looked in the mirror at all this disfigurement, I could not believe what I saw. I imagined my face looked like the inside of my heart, bruised and broken.

From one circumstance to another, I floated. The very next day, I was standing at a phone booth with a friend who was calling his connection. As the connection pulled up, my back was turned to him. I could hear the flirtatious remarks but was too ashamed to turn around. As my friend explained my dilemma to his connect, to my surprise, he asked for a date to the movies. I was stunned because I was very disfigured, so I accepted. As that evening came, Pat arrived on time, just as he said. We left, but we never made it to the movies. Instead, he took me home, gave me some changing clothes, and said I was welcome to heal here. It had been so long since anyone had been even a little kind in those streets that I let my guards down and opened my heart. When I awoke, I heard voices in the front room. As I exited to go to the bathroom, my ex was sitting there copping from Pat. I was so scared and wanted to scream, but Pat spoke gently and said they were about to leave. In that instance, that beast that rendered so much hurt to me was powerless to even speak. Pat knew exactly who he was; he just wanted me to know he was not the gangster he pretended to be. He was just another coward, a womanizer. A loser who could only whip a woman.

As I began to venture outside, I stumbled into trouble. That had always been my middle name. I decided to surprise Pat by moving some of his products. This game was new to me, so I was not ready. After making a few moves that day, I was on my way in for the evening, talking with the cousin of the man who blacked my eye. Whatever call she made that day, I found myself at gunpoint being robbed. A chain that Pat had given me, my first true gift from a man, and all the money I had made that day. Now I am afraid again; what is he going to do to me? As he approached to discover what had happened, he was angry but not violent. So now I have really let my guard down. To trust, to try and love as ridiculous as that seemed for me.

Then the obvious occurred; another woman showed up. His sister let her in. They lived above him. So, we are both sitting here, waiting for him to return. Like a coward, he did not. His mother came and asked if one of us could leave. "Please don't wait to ambush my son," she said. So, I left. Hurt, but I left. With nowhere to go, I finally went to my mother's. Despite how I felt about her, somehow, I could see in her face she was now sorry. She just could not reach me, for all the anger and hate I was feeling from my childhood always resurfaced. So, we rarely said too much to each other; however, I noticed she was reading her Bible. At that time, it did not mean much, but later in life, it would mean everything.

She would pray for me when I did not want to pray for myself. She believed in me when I had given up on becoming anything that had nothing to do with hustling. They say the prayers of the righteous availed much. But what would one consider righteous?

As seasons would usher in, the knowledge about the weights of cocaine took precedence over everything. Selling dope had become the norm. The problem with this is I now had a son that I protected in my own way. I took him to my mother when I ran the streets, and I would show up out of nowhere and take him shopping and give him hugs and kisses and would be gone in the streets a couple of days later. I was running from my demons, and the woman I despised was picking up the slack, trying to do better with her grandchildren than life allowed her to with her own.

By this time, I was lost. I would become a victim of circumstance. I got caught up with a group of people who somehow confused the principles that GD was built on. There were a group of girls and a group of guys, and the woman with the power to protect those women was exploiting them. First Lady Deanna. As she told me that I had to have sex with all those guys, I refused. She threatened to violate me, but that was cool. For the first time in my life, I could say no. So that was what I did. After I was let go, I had this awful taste in my mouth; I was filled with anger all over again. Then, by a moment of chance, I met a man who would change my life. I refer to him as YJ. He controlled the city at this time. He was the center of attention. After talking for what seemed like hours about the true vision Larry Hoover had for the nation for women, my understanding opened just a little. And just like that, magic was created. She was to be a face and a voice for women of that struggle, to ensure that what happened to me would never happen to another sister of the struggle. The acting first lady was removed from that power; it was turned over to me, just without a title. The work I was supposed to do and the sisters I was supposed to try and reach would dictate what I would be called.

I would come to love a board of men who had taken poverty and defeat and produced laws that would uplift a nation of people. After living with so much hurt and seeming so helpless, I now had the strength of a nation to back me. I just did not understand how much power that would entail. The knowledge of the blueprints I began to consume like nursery rhymes to children. When this knowledge began to become a part of my life, it covered up the brokenness. So, at nineteen years old, my life would grow to receive and accept death, love, hurt, confusion, and betrayal all over again.

It was too much power for a girl so young and so broken. Nevertheless, I needed the attention; I became attracted to it. It was the only thing that seemed normal to me. Like a magnet, I was drawn to it. In my mental state, I was a time bomb ticking. It would take the organization to make me aware of my self-worth over the years. Not all was pretty. I do not think it ever will be where there is violence. I began to fellowship, make money on the block, and laugh. I had not realized the seriousness of my surroundings. We were young; we were GD. We represented as such so much till we chased someone off the block for selling in our territory. I lived on this block. So, this night, as the shootout took place, I went in, and everyone scattered. But early that morning, as you came to sit out on the porch and noticed that five-o was so deep, you began to communicate and reach out to each other. You discover that the fifteen-year-old boy who came on the block to work every day after school for that measly two hundred dollars a week would no longer be coming again. He was a victim of the retaliation of the war over a stupid block that did not belong to anyone. To go and look in his mother's eyes, to see the hope for her son's future struck down by circumstance. That was not what I had read in the blueprint. We were supposed to be growing and developing past the state of poverty we were in.

This would be my first loss in the struggle, but certainly not my last. My mom had grown to love the younger brother as well. These days, she was not overbearing; she was only glad I was home more. As the rain fell that evening, tears sprinted down my face over and over. This would be the first time in years that I would talk to God. The God that I claimed was silent. I was now hoping to hear from him. I did not understand the intruder named death. Everyone I knew was dying. How do you live with that? Violence is a different beast. Dealing with the folks I knew; I would come to learn that being a part of the same organization does not make you friends.

I learned this when I chose to fall in love with TD. He was a gangster with a slot. I had come to meet him, and a brother named Boo D. He opened a door for me and put a nice quantity of narcotics in my hands. Currently, I am still naive to this game. However, I am learning to survive it. I am now meeting so many heavy hitters because of the newly gained position in the mob; relationships came and went. I was still numb and broken deep down. But TD understood me. My past came up in our relationship. The date rape I got caught up in was now being thrown up in his face, and the title slut was stamped on my back. I did not have the power to stop the ordeal. Only one person in that room chose not to violate me while I was so helpless. I looked TD in the eyes and told him there was an automatic weapon in the premises. I would not deny the situation. But how it was explained was trash. The slap on the back low-life men gives each other to seem important. I was not ready to die or wind up in a garbage can. So, I survived and lived with that embarrassment for a long time. Now, it was haunting my relationship that I had come to cherish.

Somehow, TD was able to look over it. So, I would spend my days in fantasy land, always searching for the right card to give him, the right song to play. When we touched each other, I forgot all the pain that a lot of men had caused. He was my little piece of happiness for a season. And then one rainy night, as I waited and waited for him to come and see me, I began to get impatient... I could not go to him. I was under house arrest from a pending drug case. He called me and said he was finally on his way. So, when the doorbell rang, I was full of smiles. But it was not him. It was his security telling me he had been shot. I ran out of the house and headed to the hospital as if I had no monitor on my leg.

After what seemed like ages, the inevitable happened. He was pronounced dead, and all that love I knew was gone. He accepted me as broken as I was. He loved the hurt away. My friend was gone. August 28, 1991. My dreams were now shattered. As I was allowed to leave the house, I visited his mother; she wanted to meet the woman who wrote all that poetry to her son. He had saved every card I had ever given him. She just held on to me as if she loved me because she knew I was in love with her son. The funeral I would take hard. And hatred I would create inside another. I was here in love with TD but had another person caught up in his feelings for me. Lil C. would have no idea why I was grieving so hard. We had been together for a minute, but between his job and his position in the nation, he left me alone so much that I grew to love one another. That is what confusion is like. I am attracted to it somehow.

As time passed, no one noticed this tomb of reckless emotions. They only saw the beauty and spunk of the actor I had become. The GD's Magic. Loved by many and hated by some. The disturbing part is what one considers love. An intimate love, a true connection in spirit where you only want what is best for the other. Or is it the way a person performs for the night and pulls out that big old bag of tricks that she shares in her moment of weakness? Or is it the way her smile lights up in a room of angry and violent aggressors? Or is it the way she humbles her mind to offer idiotic compassion to men who would never offer honesty, motivation, or even a listening ear in a time of need? Still figuring out the definition of love and its outrageously recorded angles documented by the psychologist who pretends to have the answers to the bullshit we call and assume is love.

Then comes the direct opposite, the hatred people carry, invented by explanations one gives themselves in justification. Hating magic for finally thinking she is cute, hot, smart, and attractive. For believing she is caring and domineering. Hating herself for surviving. For trying to change and see the world through different eyes, even with the blurred visions from her past. I think one of the strongest hates I ever endured was being hated because I survived life's intended tragedy. Death was now playing with me. It started to reach out and contact me personally. It is closer than ever before. On November 28, 1994, I watched my lover fight the Grim Reaper. His will to live was so strong that he cursed in hellish words. As he fought for life, I could see the pain in his eyes as the bullets bombarded his body. I like to remember the Panther G sharp as the man he was. The father that death stole from so many. A lover struck down by hate and jealousy. When you got cowards cooperating with the Feds, they find fault with people. Maybe He had some; all I know is what I remember.

Chapter Nine

Death Does Leave Scars

THE BIGGEST BULLY I had ever faced was death. A galloping intruder, he dances within the realm of my thoughts and saddens my soul. Like an unannounced tornado, death ripped open my heart, leaving me in sheer agony. Tons of questions with no answers. He never warned me of his arrival. He only left his autograph as he departed.

In the early '90s, I had read many articles in the Chicago area. Being a part of the Gangster Disciples, I felt a need to understand the violence in the street that was reported to be gang related. I once seemed to comment on the outcomes of these events as if maybe the victims could have done things differently. During this process, I sometimes made public appearances at the funerals of associates and their family members. Respect. Having a position had its prices that needed to be paid in those days.

Accepting death was one of them. It was no different from falling soldiers or officers. We love our own. I discovered that death had the strength to paint pictures in the minds of people. I just never knew how deep. When I would visit the bereaved, I would tell them how God's time is not ours or that their loved one has moved on to a better place. I have also insinuated on many occasions that time heals all wounds.

Chapter Ten

A Thing That I Differ on Today

OVER THE UPCOMING years, death would rape me repeatedly. It constantly visited people in my circle. This again demanded my presence at many journeys of loved ones and of people who were guiding lights in the later development of my life. People who mentioned endless possibilities to dreams. One person I had come to know was Charles Ray, Larry Hoover's brother. Charles Ray believed that I could become a successful speaker in politics concerning nation business. He also encouraged my writing. I was so undeveloped, but I had a lot to say. I had prepared political speeches to reach my people. The GDs, the community. It was my designated duty as we positioned ourselves for Change. I needed to become politically aware, so I mimicked Operation PUSH. Watched how Jessie moved and even listened to him speak. I saw political figures grow in power as the man who supported their movements lay forgotten by these politicians. Where Larry Hoover could share words of wisdom in support of these politicians, he did. Somehow, after a rise to a senate seat, he becomes long forgotten to my knowledge. Allah knows best.

Finally, at twenty-three, I would come face to face with my tormentor. I and my unborn child's father sat waiting in traffic as a red light came on in our direction. We were waiting in this intersection on the Kostner exit on the West Side of Chicago. Our situation had been strained, and we had spent some time apart. I had left town to sort out my situation. Pregnancy would bring me back. As we sat there, we laughed. So much time had passed, and life had to get back on track. It is just at this moment we were racing against our fates and did not even know it. On this cold and wet day, we would come to know death up close and personal. Death would change lives forever.

During the moments of those peaceful smiles that were hard to come by these days, there rang out a sound that I had not heard in a long time. In that brief moment of peace, gunshots filled the air from so many different directions. Broken glass flew everywhere. In seconds, that peace I had witnessed was stolen. In desperation, I glanced over to witness the anguish in Panther's eyes as his body was bombarded with multiple gunshots. As moments passed, I would feel the same fiery sting. A piercing piece of steel had ripped open the flesh of my arm and broken it. As more bullets continued to soar through the air in our direction, Panther leaned over from his seat and shielded my body from the remainder of the gunshots. After a while, there was complete silence. There now lay a body so heavy on top of me that I was having trouble breathing.

I was still afraid shooters were near, so as he groaned, I quietly whispered they might shoot some more. But the shooters disappeared as fast as they appeared. Hearing the radio of the police, I yelled for help; this body that had just saved my life was now crushing my child. As they pulled him off me, I heard him curse, so

I assumed he would be okay. As I was being lifted in the ambulance, I looked and saw GDs in my peripheral. I wondered how they could be here so fast. As I made it to the hospital, I was wheeled into a room where I looked down to see Panther's boots. I could hear them trying to revive his body. I screamed, "Is he okay? Please, somebody tell me." Instantly, the doctor ordered me to be moved. I later learned they were afraid I would go into shock and cause myself to deliver our child early. Shortly after, they told me he was pronounced dead at 4:38 p.m.

I could not wrap that around my subconscious. This could not be happening to me. I was pregnant. He was the father. I had no answer at this moment. Moments later, a close friend of Panther's came into the ER. He asked what happened. I said our own people shot us. I was instructed to never mention that statement again. He told me if I needed him, he would be there. He loved him as well. That night, it rained so hard. I was so hurt, and a close friend showed up at the hospital and said, "Let's go. Do not give them a chance to finish this." I had to put years of distrust to the side. I left with Shanell. She was the only one I told what had really happened to me. She never betrayed me. She took care of me until the funeral. But after, I was shell-shocked, and I ran from place to place. I even spent a night at the house of the ole man's sister (Dianne). Dianne showed me so much kindness, especially with me being a stranger to her. My son and I were safe there for the moment.

As the tears ran frantically down my face, a hurt I have still not been able to define filled my heart. I was now calling out to God. He was the only one capable of knowing my heart. Death had come face to face with me again. He left me on display. This broken shell of a woman. Fragile and incomplete. So undefined by life. As the days kept passing, people would say how I had beaten my tormentor. I survived death's rage. Many people call this a miracle and a blessing.

However, at this time, I felt defeated, abandoned, and battered. My unborn child and I were granted an extension in life, while my lover and captive was denied inhaling and exhaling the air of the universe. The air we take for granted each day. We were robbed of any future compassion from the lover I once feared but grew to love. He would never see my child take her first breath and walk her first steps, watch her blossom to womanhood, or ever know her siblings. Every obligation to my child now rested solely with me and God. It was death's reminder of his power, his pain, and his torture, the crumbs left by death's time clock. That week yielded so much pain. I had also discovered that Danny Price and Crip were killed as well, all in that same week. Every individual I had once loved. I was now dealing with the rumor that I was a black widow. Men I loved were disappearing. That was always the fate and luck I carried early on in life.

Chapter Eleven

The Search

LOOKING BACK AT that chaos, I am sitting here today remembering what it was I needed. I lacked a father figure who could guide me to my promise land. The land where I could be free mentally. I sat here remembering the chairman's advice: "Go to school, magic. You have time for children later when you are financially stable. Education and economics tend to go together. You need them both to establish yourself on solid ground." Listening to the old man brought comfort. I felt important even within the constraints of life. And like a father, he and Winndye were there at times.

I was doing a three-year prison bit. Somehow, the old man had my lawyers paid on a case that did not have anything to do with our involvement. And when Christmas came, Winndye sent money for my books and a card. That was more than my blood kin had done. I will always love them for that. I will love them for believing in me when I did not believe in myself. Larry was just a father who cared for the youth. He taught me that I did not have to go to the military to be all I could be. I just needed to live up to my full potential. I just needed to discover it. He and the board had already given us the blueprints to life. The star I loved so much represented the virtues of love, life, loyalty, wisdom, knowledge, and understanding. To gain understanding, you must first discover who you are. Love yourself past the mistakes. As I began to understand that God had been with me all through my life, when I was being preyed on, he gave me the strength of endurance. Those lessons would create a strong woman in time. I just could not see it for many years.

Chapter Twelve
The Quest

I WENT OUT ON a quest searching for the man who would complete me from within. On that journey, I discovered it was not his place to do so.

The answers lay within the shattered fragments of my past and all the burdens and lessons I persevered through; this was my prison because I let it control me.

First, be true to thyself. I failed here. I wore the mask that signaled happiness for a season; when reality presented its case, I was empty inside and out. Without any spiritual comfort, I was committing a mental suicide, overdosing on regrets.

Diving right back into that ocean of tears I had dropped over the years; I was sending out this confusion into the universe. When God forgives you, it is settled. I just kept picking up the same shackle, dragging it from place to place.

In this quest, I questioned my significant others' failure to mend the brokenness, a brokenness that only I can come to terms with. In the back of my mind, I am staring at this piece of a man, realizing this is why I married several times. I am the only one who has the power to produce my happiness. I must love myself more than the definition one has for the ideal woman. My self-worth must be greater than monetary value. I just needed to believe it. Claim it.

I started off by looking at myself in the mirror and saying, "You are beautiful. You are the design that God chose to produce. You do not need a man's approval to be complete. You need God, and in his time, He will send you your mate. Quit searching for the tangible. Have a little *sabir* (Arabic for "Patience"). In the Bible, you only needed a mustard seed of faith; in Quran, you know to call on him by his attributes. *Ya Allah, Ya Allah, Ya Allah.*" But stubbornness keeps man from crying out to the only healer: God. He and only He can send you the compatible mate. Equal Yoke. With mutual love and respect.

REMINDERS

WATCHING MY LIFE and its accomplishments, I stare at the mirror. I remember a surah in Quran, in Al- 'Asr: "By the token of time through the ages, verily man is in loss, except such as have faith, and do righteous deeds, and join together in mutual teaching of truth, and of patience and constancy."

I have been to the bottom, and God has allowed me to rise to the top. I assumed that with success, I would be happy; I was wrong. I am happier with servitude. Trying to sow some good seeds despite the past. To the world, GDs are placed in a category that defines us as nonproductive. I beg to differ. The world can ban Christmas for over one hundred years. But in the same breath today, there came back a spiritual-based play, and I love it despite the evil that St. Nicholas caused. But Mr. Hoover, a man of intellect, wisdom, and atonement, can receive not one sympathetic gesture. I looked back at the politicians who raped the African American communities for our support. They could and did reckon with this man of intellect in the need to be elected. Farther down the line, they disassociated themselves. The question I ask the most is why. The old man is still the beacon who wants change, who wants to educate the youth.

Share with the under-privileged adults and protect the old. These are the simple duties we find many Muslims are trying to achieve. Can we forgive a mask murderer but not a man who lost his freedom in his youth? A man who spent a decade trying to change lives. The GD organization did not fail me. I failed it. I learned to become a voice to be reckoned with later than intended. I chose to deviate from the teachings and find my own way. The journey was long and painful. But that was my choice; I accept that. It was different from the cowardice of many men who would blame their mischievous actions on a man who was not even present. It was strange, so I found it to be hypocritical of our government to allow Mr. Hoover to be charged on such allocation, especially when soldiers in South Sudan personally abused and violated human rights. This happened around July of 2016. It is thirty-one pages long. But not once did the word *conspiracy* slip from anyone's lips. Throughout history, we explain away the government's faults but find laws and legal loopholes to attack the African American community. (For American readers, investigate to see how much property was seized when the GD organization was divided.) What bank accounts were liquidated? You will find that the punishment was never defended by any proof. Just deals our police make with stories from their informants that may not contain any truth. It happened in Texas, and it happened right under our noses in Chicago. With age comes wisdom; I now try and defend the weak and protect the orphan. Teach a skill that can gain you a job that pays decent wages. Give back to the community with the tools the blueprints I studied have outlined. We never asked America to give us any fish; we only wanted to learn how to fish. Instead, they locked up the Black men and kept them from raising their children. I do not think we got a brief break until families of multi races began to form. God had somehow, for a second, given prejudice a black eye. That is the beauty of Islam. There is no color nor race to sisters and brothers trying to bring unity and hope to share a way of life for national peace. I fight hard to be a sister of the Struggle who changed and evolved. A sister who set aside her prejudice to grasp a dream that there is still hope for humanity. If I can just touch one life, that one life, in return, may touch two. Inshallah, a domino effect will occur, and we will teach each other to love and not hold on to hatred. It will destroy you. I know firsthand. After I had begun to heal, I never just held my mother tight and told her how much I had come to know about the depths of her love. She was always trying to make up for one mistake. Repeatedly.

I, in my selfishness, never gave her that satisfaction. One day, she called me, and I was busy running my nightclub. I told her I would call her back. A shoot-out occurred that night, and I closed early. I did not call her though. I went to another club owner's establishment, returning about 4:00 a.m. When my phone rang that morning, my little brother/ first cousin kept trying to find the words to tell me that my mother fell dead after a stroke. All I could think of was she was waiting for me to call her back. She had been waiting on me for over twenty years just to tell her I loved her. And I did. I was just too stubborn to let her know. I assumed little gifts here and there for her would suffice. Now she was gone.

It would not be enough to heal that hole I did not allow to mend. I just kept on making her relive her mistakes. Asking God to forgive me but never fully lifting that burden from my mother's chest. The woman who drove from Mississippi to Chicago to get me when I got shot. The woman who helped raise my children when I was running the streets. The woman who only wanted to see that smile I used to give her as a child. That is the burden I will have to bear. I imagine when I stand before God, the angels will ask me why I did not give forgiveness when God gave it to me repeatedly. So, into the universe, I say my apologies and my prayers for her while she is in her grave to not fall on deaf ears from God. A remarkable woman who loved so many so hard and paid too much for the love she got in return. *I love you so much, Mama. I wish you were here. I just know that is one wish that will never come true. But I love you, nonetheless.*

MOTHER

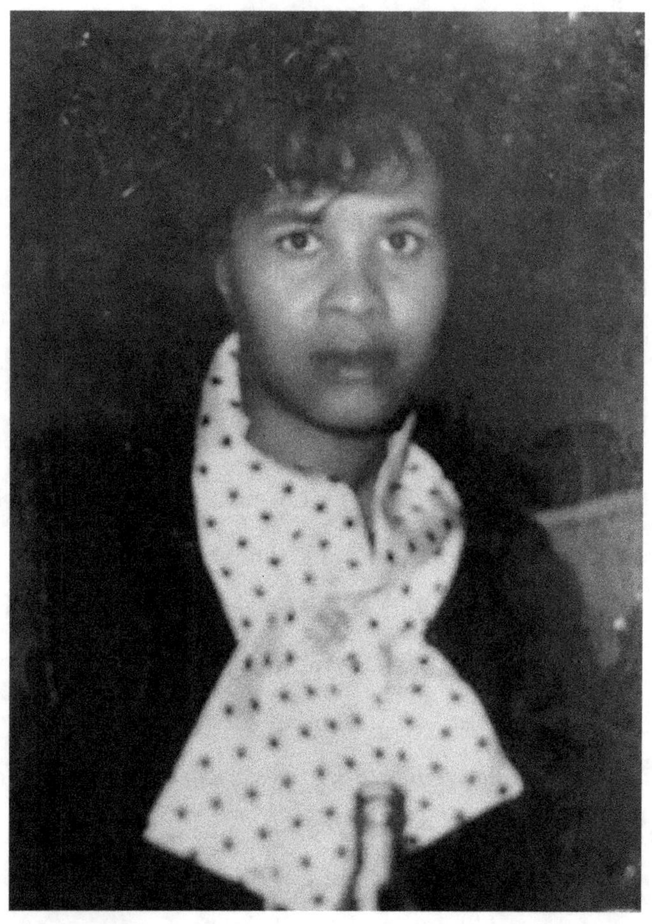

HERE ARE NO number of words that can describe the woman you grew to be. Always studying your Bible and watching me go back and forth in life, griping about a time that had passed.

Always stopping me before I leave your home, asking me to bow my head in prayer just in case seeing me that day could be your last.

Trying to share what you had come to discover in your last days on this earth, trying to make me see that it was no accident that you allowed my birth. It was a choice.

Oh, how I miss her every hour of my day, Lord; my mother has been swept away. I pray for forgiveness, and if it is in your divine will for her to rest in peace, please grant her that. I am just asking for forgiveness because she never got too much peace from me.

I encourage the world to look around and honor their mother and father, just as has been written. I also encourage children, teenagers, and battered women to reach out and tell someone. It is truly a hard concept to swallow. I know. For me, after analyzing my family tree, I came to learn that pain had lurked within my family through the ages. My great-grandmother, who I am told believed in the black arts, stopped my grandmother from being able to be loved by my grandfather. My mother went through quite an ordeal because of family choices. My mother was just as broken as I was. I just never knew her pain. However, life has allowed me to taste it.

I accept doing seven years and nine months in federal prison. My children have the right to be angry. I sent them money from prison jobs; I sent the angel tree at Christmas. I wrote and sent cards and blankets so they would know they were loved. I wanted to change the pattern my family has with communication. So, when I was released from prison, I came home working straight from the halfway house. My dream to put my family back together was all I had, and it was my only goal in life at that time. I begged, borrowed, and schemed to send my daughter to prom and drive her to college.

But circumstances would still try and break my will. People claiming to be Christians befriended my child, and at age twenty, they convinced her to do an adult adoption. They created a motion and took her to the court here in Minnesota, paid a fee, and changed her birth certificate. My name is no longer on that birth certificate. I was broken, and I was angry. Me being Muslim, I had plenty to say about the church. But then, I realized it was not Christianity that tricked my child into doing this. These were people claiming to be Christians. I took some time to heal from this. I had been trying to make up for so much that I was just giving all that I had. Most were advice and any funds I had. But sometimes, little girls need more.

I started by accepting that I did not go to prison for my children. I could have worked three jobs and been there. I had to accept my own mistakes and make peace with them, or the devil was going to trick me again. So spiritually, I tried to be a good Muslim, but I am not without flaw. That is where the devil attacks and tricks you. Falling should never be the problem; lying there and not getting back up should. I fought to be reckoned with the only way I knew how.

I went back to school. I took culinary arts; I opened my catering company, and a Black Minnesota judge gave me all my rights back. I would like to say that he was all I needed, but I would be lying to the people I want to help. My white probation officer hounded me so much until he saved me from myself. I was surely about to drown. I use the separation in the words *white* and *black* to merely give an example about groups of people who all had my best interests at heart, but the description separated their actions.

Their actions were the same; words separate and confused. Today, I stand before you to say that all lives matter; but there is a disparity in the number of African American lives that are lost because of gun violence, police brutality, and fear of the color of their skin. I have this fear. The fear that no matter how hard I attempt to be a good Samaritan or how many lives I try and save, the world will ignore all the good to hold on to the darkest moment at your weakest point.

GROWING OLDER THERE WAS ONCE a time when I assumed that time was all I needed. Time to heal, time to find peace. I assumed that when I went to prison, I could do that time; I was strong enough. My family appeared to be intact. Be careful of your words to God about an unknown future. I thought my father would hold me down during these dark days. We were at odds. I protected the man I thought was the father of my child to protect my father. We were dealing with the Feds. I could not implicate anything without it becoming a conspiracy. Conspiracy Also known as a plot. A secret plan or agreement through persons. The word can be used positively or negatively. We conspire every day to feed the homeless, create Covid relief. What is the sentence? Should there be when something goes wrong? It is just a word.

Chapter Thirteen

The Wisdom of Larry

THERE WAS A question posed by Larry Hoover: Do you know why people join gangs?

Why? Because gangs are the social clubs of the ghetto; people want to belong to something.

From the eyes of a broken woman, I would have to agree. The organization gave me purpose, made me a part of a family. No different from social media; everyone wants to be a part of a page in someone's life. I became a part of Growth and Development.

Chapter Fourteen

Clean Up

I REMEMBER WHEN IT started. My mom had just died. I was grieving so bad that I stayed up days sniffing powder cocaine, functioning without anyone really knowing how bad I was. I wanted to give up. The burden of my mother's death was too hard to bear, the state our relationship was in when she passed. One night, I had gotten so high that I broke down and told God I just cannot live in these conditions anymore. Prayed to come down off that trip. I was a wreck. Then God answered those prayers. The Feds raided me a few days later. I was now on a case, and I knew I was going to prison. My only option was to snitch on Dad. Not an option. He was mad at me because I did not tell on the dude either. There would be no conspiracy with me. I gave my father half of every sale he set up for me. I ran that nightclub, and I gave my stepmom every dime I made off it. I took care of my children on the crumbs left over from a low-paying job in Mississippi and the split between me and my dad.

I protected their land and property, a property that never benefited me or my children. During my first year of prison, my father got shot and killed at seventy-one years old. My aunt Helen died, my uncle Ben died, my aunt's baby Kae died. My stepmom came down with Alzheimer's disease. So, it was just me and God.

He was all I had. Many times, I could not even call my children on holidays because the man I kept silent about left me before I was to turn myself in. Sometimes, when everyone leaves you, it is a good thing. Now God had the floor in my life. As fast as I got my prison sentence, deadbeat fathers started filing for custody of my children to keep from paying child support. I had no life, I thought, for many seasons.

I had to remind myself that God is always there. I studied the Bible with an academy through mail from Joplin, Missouri. I studied the Catholic Bible; I studied the Torah, and they all led me to Islam. Now I could understand my separation from my family and the distance I had from God. I never knew the miracles. I never knew about all the mercies God gave. So, as I began to pray five times a day, I began to read and write Muslim pen pals. I found peace and an abundance of love. I started to walk five miles a day to have time to talk to God, to accept my losses. I remembered something my father said in our last conversation. He said, "Baby, this can only get better; you are at the bottom now. There is no other place for you to go but up." We were at odds because I did not tell on the guy in my life and take the deal. He never understood.

If I tell on my guy, I might as well tell on him. That was the door that would open.

He was not sending me money. I cried just a little. I

remember the roommate I had was there because her daughter told on her. They had money. Exquisite lounges and limos. The whole family went down. Her daughter had turned on her. She took a deal and sent her parents to prison. As we exchanged stories, she said she wished I were her daughter. You would have wanted nothing in here. She protected me in her own way; I was pregnant when I got locked up. It happened after I made a bond. I spent a great many years locked up there with her; I watched her break down. Her life had slipped away from her. She came down with Alzheimer's disease and finally passed away. Before she became ill, she was a beast though.

And those were the lessons God needed me to see. People were dying in prison. Cancer patients were leaving for surgeries and dying on the table. The woman who prepared my legal work died before she would ever see me give some time back. The Feds put you in contact with people from all social classes. So many lifers or people with twenty years or better. I have heard and read some cases. Death somehow humbles a person's heart. I was always afraid of dying in prison and my death certificate reading "escape by death." I cannot imagine the families who received those death certificates. Today, I live my life for people who never got another chance to try and get it right.

I live my life for Reggie because his stopped at fifteen. I now strive to live my life with purpose.

I grew over the last quarter of a century. I have developed into an understanding mom and a citizen who works hard and pays her taxes. I grew up to represent what true growth and development were supposed to look like. I was a child when I accepted my cause, now that I try to make good on my beliefs as I see the gray.

Chapter Fifteen

Time

WATCHING TIME MOVE forward faster than you ever thought it possible as a child is one of the most challenging feelings of all.

As gray approaches and your knees begin to buckle in prayer, you find yourself running out of the moments once deemed possible.

In a race for time, you lose sight of the future, and you learn to embrace the here and now. You recount the words of God and the hadiths as they warned the signs you see when the end is near.

Death does not sneak up without a warning. Early on, I was not so sure about this. Looking around, I see the signs that God gives to man. We just ignore them; it is the way of some of the children of Adam.

Out of all the regrets I have had in life, domestic violence has been one of my weakest states. I wondered how screwed up I must have been to end up loving Panther. He seemed so calm when I met him.

Despite the rumors about him and the way he lived his life, I still toyed with the friendship. He was there when I was doing my three-year state prison bit. He purchased shoes and various things for me when I was away, mainly because I associated myself with the GDs from out West when I was convicted on that case. I am not sure how I let him get so close to me after release. He never visited me in prison. It was T., the walking bible of knowledge. He came to visit me in Dwight. He came so late that the visit was like fifteen minutes, and then he had to go. Prison was new for me. I broke down in tears as he was instructed to leave. Like a loyal friend and gangster, he promised he would be back next week.

When the next week came, he was there. He left me money and was a true support until I blew it. It is what Magic does, get caught up in the moment. They moved me to Logan Correctional Center, and that's how Panther got into my life. He had given orders for those sisters to listen to me as I spoke about what the vision was outside those walls. I got so caught up in the power that I became so loose in my actions. It was a coed prison, so I reached out to a couple of prominent guys.

Boo and J.D were there. Somewhere, it was a disconnect from the Lows and Englewood. I performed in talent shows and worked my magic. To see Boo. I even got my GED, which would be everything later in life. The sexy men seemed to be in college. That is where I was trying to be. Being a GD, our people was in place. Got them library passes to see my people in the flesh. This is where Boo and I would heal. We were always at odds with each other. I believe it was the attraction I had for him and something he may have felt for me. Our circumstances never let me become a part of his life.

Instead, I got released and hit that brutality and the beast that was lying dormant in Panther. We talked so much like friends until I was released from the halfway house. Panther offered to pick me up, and I consented. I had no idea what would be waiting for me. We made rounds in areas, which seemed normal to me as a board member. What was not normal was the visit to the Cabrini-Green projects. As we arrived, out of nowhere, this beast just began to slap me around. He was a big guy. I dare not even try to fight back; he was a board member. No one could help me. They were scared. He had slapped me around so much I lost my diamond earrings. He made the folks look for them. They were mad at me because it would be their ass if they did not find them.

After, I was just waiting for my moment to disappear, like magic. He did not let that happen. He made me go everywhere he went all day till the next day, modern-day kidnapping. Finally, he had to go see the man. It would have been a good escape, but he told his security and his follower Ty to keep an eye on me until he came back. Ty hated being put in that position, but it was the law that day. But he tried to be humane. He said, "Look, Magic, I do not want to get put in a trick bag. So, I am going to trust you to move around. Do not get me jammed up." So, I could have run and let Ty feel Panther's wrath for letting me out of his sight. But I did not. I knew what that hurt felt like from that beating, and I did not want to cause any more harm. These were the types of acts the ole man wanted to prevent. I was too afraid and too ashamed to speak out. I just played the position by his side until I could play it no more. After being with him and knowing how long he had been locked up, I understood how he could force himself to be with me sexually in ways that a young woman would feel inhumane. As time passed, I realized that I was with a child. I was angry; I did not want a baby with this man.

So, I finally got a message from the only one I thought could help me, and he did. The ole man told me I could leave. I am not sure what type of relationship or bad blood, if any, this caused. I was sure that the ole man was a protector of the weak. I left the state. I took some time to digest my situation, knowing that if I gave this child life, it was going to forever change mine. I wondered how many beatings may occur during his right to see his child. My life was a wreck. After choosing to do what is right by my child, I decided not to terminate the pregnancy. The baby was still a part of me. After many months went by, it was time to face reality. I did not have money, I was with a child, and I missed home. I was raised in Chicago; I was just a native of Mississippi.

It was time to go back. So, I returned after the long separation. We talked about the time I was away. Everyone thought the pregnancy was a lie. He knew the truth because of the ultrasound.

When I arrived in the city that morning, I contacted him and let him know I was back. For some strange reason, he sounded shaken. He asked me where I was. After finding out, he immediately came to me. When he saw me, I was showing very much in the pregnancy. He looked in my eyes and said, "You should not be here. Things have changed. You cannot trust people." Then he touched my stomach and said, "But you are here now. I got you. I am so sorry." He said he will never put his hands on me again. He said, "You are afraid of me. I have broken your will. If I do that, you are not a person with your own thoughts. You are a robot, and I need you. Willingly." It was hard for me to even think about what he was saying. It was so unlike him. He said he must get me a new place and a car to get around. And we exited. He had security, but on this day, he just wanted to spend some time with me. Time we would never see.

So that was how it ended for us. He died saving my life. It was a hit. Sounds so funny coming from my mouth and it not being on TV. I always imagine what life would have looked like for me. Would I have become a pattern of domestic abuse, or would he have kept his word for the sake of our child? I will never know. I do not think it matters. She now knows how he died. We will never know why. I do not want to know. I try not to dwell on how Panther lived his life. I try and dwell on the fact that a man has lived. He has left me the best part of himself. He was broken and damaged. He never denied that. He told me how his mother treated him. Be it the truth or a lie, I never searched for them. I have loved my child as hard as a mother can.

I looked in her face and saw gestures that looked like some of those looks he would give.

So, I had to love her harder. I had to embrace her and remind myself she was my child, and no amount of abuse would ever change that. One day, we cried together so hard. She had found the news articles of the shooters' appeals and what was said. I could now see the betrayal, the people who called the hit and executed it. No remorse for innocent bystanders being in the car. Selfish, just wanting to hit the target. There were so many cars out that day. Just firing, never wondering what kind of damage those stray bullets could have caused. Just twenty-five minutes earlier, my six-year-old son was in that car. I do not know how I would have reacted had he been hurt. I am grateful to God my son is still alive. So as the tears fell from my eyes, my daughter just kept saying, "Mama, I am sorry. I should not have looked at them. I am sorry." But she was not wrong; I should have told her the truth. Instead, I needed her to have a piece of happiness to hold on to. So, I never talked about how we met, how she came to be, but only how he saved her life. That was all that mattered.

Chapter Sixteen

Clarity

PEOPLE WONDER HOW I can feel so partial about the struggle with all my chaotic episodes. To open a vision, to understand, I would have to compare it with the Bible. Job was tested hard, but he was still faithful. Moses never the saw the promised land, but he loved God. God never caused the pharaoh to challenge Moses. Pride did. I know. The ole man never sanctioned so many actions. Man chose to do what he wanted. So many were what I called hypocrites. Even I, for what it was worth. The old man said, "Magic, it's okay. Go." I came back. I confused my situation with a need to be in the predicament at that moment.

So many sisters of domestic abuse make the same mistake as I did. Their outcomes sometimes have been and will be worse if they do not make better choices than the ones I made.

When a man is broken and he hits you the first time, do not be fooled; he will hit you again. It is in him. By the second time, he will become more comfortable. And by the third, he will have formed a habit, a habit to break your will. Keep your self-esteem low. If you have small children, they will grow to despise the weakness—not their mom but the character she displays. God never intended for a woman to be a punching bag. We were to be a comfort and garment to our mate. Our friendship was to be close and honorable. In Islam, 50 percent of our worship is to try and make our marriage work, which helps in our servitude to God. We rear children who are believing men and women of God. This is my greatest challenge. My patience with the male species is short. Abuse can cause a mental separation from your emotions. I love, but I never stay there. I trust but only so far. This is what God has to heal. As you find your path to your growth and develop into the woman God has intended you to be, there must come about change. Nothing stays the same. Flowers are seeds, then buds, and then beautiful blooms.

But it changes in stages. Your life and your worship must change too. During what seemed to be one of my most difficult experiences, the humbleness was the hardest to cultivate. When I think about all the times, I heard my mother speak about God, I remember being so convinced mentally about hypocrisy. I could not open up and let the words she shared in. Abuse and bitterness were always my separation. Now I am sitting here in prison with ten- and eleven-month sentences. Everything around me was numb in the beginning. My son's and my daughter's cries. It was overwhelming. For many days, it was hard to call and hear them. One day in particular, my baby boy said, "Mom, if you come home, I promise to be good."

Then the *please* following it had thrown my heart against the wall.

When everyone leaves you and there is no one that you can count on, that is when a mind can be free. After all the chaos, I finally broke down and prayed. This time, prayer was different. I was purifying my mind and my body to come into communion with the creator. It is what is known as the *Niyaat* (an Arabic word meaning "intention"). As I cleared my mind and released all the hurt from hearing my children cry, all the blame for how I got there, those words he set me up with vanished. I was taking responsibility for my own actions and asking God to forgive the woman I was. I had kneeled and placed my forehead on the floor, and in that second, I began to humble myself. It was not about me or the children. It was about my relationship with God. I was spiritually bankrupt, and I needed to be free from the world as I knew it to be.

Lying there in prostration, there were no predators. Just me and God. After that prayer, I began to look at myself through different eyes. I wanted to cover up my hair, shield that glory. That is what Christians call a woman's hair. Her glory. I realized my journey was going to be long. But for the first time, I had a path to take. The more I began to read and study religions and different walks of life. I decided I wanted to take the middle course. I wanted no extremes. I tried to balance my thoughts and steer away from judgment, leaving alone that which did not concern me.

Chapter Seventeen

Skills

DURING THIS SEASON in my life, I decided to take cosmetology. It kept me motivated in preparing for my release. I spent three years going to cosmetology school in Texas. I took my boards twice, one for cosmetologist and another for cosmetology instructor. We paid the fees for our licensing. Things were great, and then right up to release, Texas decided not to honor the license they issued. They claimed they did not know the school was for inmates, and they do not give prisoners their license.

We had no money for lawyers. I had managed to reciprocate with West Virginia before they took them. This experience is why I have no respect for some legislations and politicians. You would think Texas would have refunded our money. Instead, I had been used again, just in a unique way. I was used by the system.

Many people get angry and lose sight. I kept pushing. I had not made this change to let it be for nothing.

Something had to come from all the hurt. And it did.

After my release, I was working low-paying temporary jobs, and I went back to college in the free world.

Whatever license I earned; we would go to court if they tried to take them now. I spent two and a half years in culinary school. I worked full-time, trying to be that parent my children needed. Then graduation came, and I had been with JW Marriott for a couple of years now. Life was starting to get brighter.

I made some mistakes during those two years, but God dispersed an angel or something because I got favor. That was not something I was used to. My probation officer had pulled me in and filed for a violation. My UA had traces of cocaine but not user levels. I was married to a guy that seemed to usher that old me back into existence. He was Muslim as well, but he had not fully submitted to Islam. I am always stumbling, and my husband was my obstacle. He was surprisingly good to me and exceptionally good to my children. He just loved hustling. My probation officer thought that I would tell my husband, but I did not. So, when court came, by a stroke of divine intervention, my husband had caught a case. Cocaine. The law protected me from ever having to speak on my husband.

So, my lawyer said if I don't have a dirty UA for six months, we would revisit this and ask the district attorney to drop the charges. It was agreed.

Six months later when court came, of course, I was scared as hell; but I was praying for a miracle. I got my SERV Safe certification and opened a small online business. Then out of nowhere, this African American judge told me to pat myself on the back. I had met the conditions to drop the charges. But he promised me in open court that if I kept trying, he would be willing to suspend all that supervised release.

For a year, I was on pins and needles thinking the probation officer was out to get me. That had been my past. Then one day, out of nowhere, he requested to see me at my home. I just knew something had come up. This time, it was different. He told me I did not need supervision anymore. Write to the judge to be released early, and he would agree. That moment moving forward, God began to change my life and heal the brokenness. There were still many lessons to come. But I saw what that probation officer had seen. I was headed back to prison. I needed his intervention. He did his job, and the result was I became a successful chef with many awards and certifications. I graduated from college, and my children can respect the woman I became. With growth and development, there will always be change.

Chapter Eighteen

Lost

I HAVE TRIED TO put every moment into the success of my children, but like the Sunna said, my children would be a test and trial for me. I struggle to give my children most of what they wanted but everything they needed, like taking student loans to buy them nice clothes. I relinquished income taxes to buy whatever the latest fashion was. Then I saw my ghost. My two youngest children just wanted to run the streets, claiming to be part of the GD. They did not get this from me. They were not even born in my day of fellowship. I would chase my twelve-year-old daughter all over Minnesota and Mississippi, trying to save her from herself. My family were like daggers in my back. The more I tried, the deeper the wound. A Families called Children and Family Services, claiming my daughter had been beaten and molested. These are church people with these lies and snares, grinning in my face and calling the hotline when I turned my back.

Minnesota family services failed my child for years. I called them for help. They would always close a case out on me. Then one day, a video of my thirteen-year-old daughter giving oral sex aired. I waited at the police departments, trying to get help, anyone who could take that video down that my confused child was fond of. I imagine karma was real. I gave up my job at JW Marriott to move back to Mississippi to save my child. I had received this offer with a 42,000 salary. I traveled all the way to Mississippi for them to take that job back because of my past. I stated I was a felon on the application. I started to take this to Supreme Court, but the Mississippi EEOC was not really looking to fight these battles. It was a right to work. People still thought eight dollars an hour is good pay.

I am not one to cry, so I was willing to take a low-paying job if I could save my child. But out of nowhere, the family I thought I had was trying to get custody. I guess a free check would do that. But my family planned against me, but God also planned. I went to court and told that judge he had jurisdiction because we were from Minnesota. He agreed after phone calls to our courts, seeing the pending court dates my daughter had. I got on the highway after sending resumes out on Indeed. Halfway back through the drive, I had been contacted for a job, and my interview was in the afternoon the next day. Edina Country Club. Just like God, I was hired, and I made the same as I made at JW Marriott. I am always grateful to JW Marriott because they offered me my job back. I just could not wait to process back in. I had been without work three weeks now, and I lost a lot relocating.

You would think my Christian family would have stopped there, but they did not. They sent for my child and bussed her back down to Mississippi, putting her at risk traveling alone. I do not blame Christianity, but I know how bold in hypocrisy its members can be. There are some in all religions. I do call a spade a spade.

I would find myself battling Mississippi again with the false allegations made by Aunt, the first lady of the church. They never really lasted long in other churches, so they brought their own, full of their children and grandchildren. Wonder why there are no members? I would hear my aunt lie about me and use their church to convince the judge on why they should get custody. But prison and that law library teach you how to fight. I simply asked the judge to ask my aunt, the first lady, why she was here filing this report instead of filing the report where the rumor said her two grandchildren, two sisters' children, are sleeping together. I thought incest was a crime. Maybe it is true, maybe it is not. But as her tears fell, she damn sure knew how I felt. After all the information about my child reached Mississippi, they now wanted to return her to the proper jurisdiction with CPS investigating me.

Bring it. When God got you, know that weapons formed against you shall not prosper. It took some time, but I finally found a social worker who read our case. She asked me to trust her. I was through with trusting people. When we met, I knew something was different. She really cared. We petitioned the court, and I had to give up my custody to get them to get my daughter Star into treatment. When a mother loves her child, she does what she got to do. My child is getting the help she needs—therapy—away from my family.

They had already done so much dirt to me; the devil could not have my child without a fight. My child was now teaching dance in treatment; she was writing poetry. She always rapped; she was a young lady with a lot to say. In time, I thought she would deliver her story. She loved me for taking her out of those noisy streets.

Now she could hear her dreams when they ask her what she wanted to be.I never thought I would spend so much time chasing my younger children, trying to help them focus on life. I assumed seeing their mother in so much pain would be enough. I was wrong.

Chapter Nineteen

Coward

I NEVER DREAMED THE first man I married would be so weak. His new wife, the one woman he had for five years while as for me he married in only five months, was bitter. The abuse my son took under that roof, I will never know how deep. All I know is he will never be the same. He will never be that little boy again. I have spent more time in court since my release than I did when I was going to jail. I remember seeing my son sobbing from the mouth from psychotropic medications when I visited him. His father was so bitter he would not let my family have our son. He forced him to stay under their roof with a jealous and bitter woman. She had her reasons in those days. Children are innocent. My son should have been off limits, but betrayal can cause many things. I often wonder how my ex-husband sleeps at night, knowing he gave me custody of our son if I would agree to never take child support. I wonder past the medications how this affected our son.

I had been hoping no one would put a bullet in him while he is lost in the world, praying and trying not to be an enabler to the life he has chosen. Then out of nowhere, the inevitable happens, he gets shot. He was in surgery for more than eight hours. His father was still such a weak man that he was not allowed to speak to me about his own son. Messages passed. Then I thought of all the turmoil his family has been through. He is already paying for being a lousy father. My children have God. They will have to come to terms and claim that for themselves. No man can bear another man's burden. They will have to surrender on their own. Sometimes I feel hypocritical. My children want to be a part of the GDs, and I do not want that for them. I beg people I know. "If you meet my child, spare them. They are not ready, and you are not ready for the mistakes they are sure to bring."

They are fighting chaos; my ashes are sprinkling in their faces. So, I ask the world I was a part of to please let them be.

It is so hard for a mother to watch her children as they stray. My methods of parenting are always considered to be wrong by my family. I am a firm and a no-nonsense woman because life will except no nonsense. My children may not get the chances I got. So, I must be this way. I remember the morning I got the call, saying they have killed my sister's son. There were no magic words for her. My entire life flashed before me. These are our babies dying in these streets. Therefore, I would rather keep my daughter in treatment than have to lower her in the dirt. I have not yet even grieved or accepted the death of my sister's son when a year later, the phone rings to tell me my other sister's son has been shot to death in the mall on Martin Luther King's birthday. Our children are not safe. Our African American children.

So again, yes, all lives matter; but the number of African American deaths has no comparison to other races. When I speak out, I can sometimes see the prejudice in faces of some Caucasian people, the stares because I am Black and Muslim. I remember having my car struck in anger by a white woman in a parking lot of the grocery store in Minnesota. I yelled for the police, so she jumps in her car and speeds away. Onlookers get the license plate. The officer comes over to tell me he did not see visible damage, and if I called my insurance, he would press charges on me. His statement was "you people always trying to use the race card." I called the police station, and a desk sergeant asked if I would come make the report and keep following up with it, so it does not fall in the cracks. This is approximately 2015. Racism is still very real. It is an even harder demon to battle when you have priors. You are always looking over your shoulder.

Chapter Twenty

Hope

THERE WAS A time when I hoped to get past the domestic abuse, to forget what a man's fist feels like, to try and forget the times you took those unwanted sexual gestures. I now am grateful for the strength to move around when violence occurs. You have one time to put your hand on me after Panther, then one of us was headed to the cemetery. So, I chose to never stay long in relationships. I imagine I never even gave a man a chance to think about if he was even in a relationship. That is what abuse caused. Physical abuse, child abuse, mental abuse. I was so angry for so long I hoped that God would allow me to accept the selfishness I caused before my mother's death. I am sure she died with a broken heart. Life did not end up the way she thought it would; what is crazy is that lousy piece of a man she married would not even come to her funeral. So, I hope now she is in peace. I hope that if I cannot help my own children, then, Lord, help me save someone else's. So many different scenes playing inside my head at one time. All bundled up waiting to escape. If there is any hope left in this world, Lord, give it to my sisters. Let them find peace during these tragedies. My sister loves God, but this tragedy has made her bitter. She cannot forgive at this time. Let her find it so she may find her way back to you.

She kept her son before you, she took him to worship, and she always taught him to love you, God. I hope she finds her way. The police department closing his death and never trying to bring anyone to justice only makes me wonder what other deal was struck to ignore the loss of life. With Black lives, another black man can take them, snitch on someone else, and walk away as if no damage has been done. Is that injustice we seek to put an end to? Has law enforcement become so lazy and quick to get a case under their belt that they can come between justice and family closure?

Chapter Twenty-One

SOS

WHEN WE OVERCAME poverty, sexual abuse, domestic abuse, being single parents, and learning to fellowship to teach another sister about survival, we became a power to be reckoned with. We learned to hold our heads up high, to forgive. It is in forgiveness we find our freedom to be sisters who overcome a struggle. I cannot speak for everyone. But I will say that past all the abuse, there were times when we fellowshipped, and life was uplifting. One of my favorite uncles is the cat in the hat. I stayed in trouble because I always brought controversy. I had learned to try and fight back, to speak out when the brothers fell short to honor our place. The cat was a serious guy but a true man of understanding. He made sure the GDs he encountered got their GEDs and respected the old people. It is the way he tried to bring together a community rather than tear it down. There will always be circumstances with which one must deal. He was a fair and just man. I once loved a figure that sat beside him not because he was so great but because he was sincere. The time he spent with my son, although life would keep it short, is moments that cannot be replaced. It is because of those times my oldest son has a respect for laws, has a respect for Tank that he will not push to the side. My son has had his trials to deal with; it is in the last bit of advice from Tank that my son would find his way. After receiving five years in the penitentiary, he now understands what Frank was saying. We choose our destiny. We can stay on the straight path, or we can lose sight of life by circumstances. Choices, everyone has choices.

For the world, when I say without the organizational structure, I would have never understood how supreme God is. Without teachings that the honorable chairman and the board put in place and someone believing in me, I may have never survived the streets of Chicago. With every difficulty, God brings ease. But I have also read that he never changes the conditions of man until he first changes the conditions of his heart. Islam was purification to me. Through understanding the Sunnah of the Prophet (PBUH), I was able to accept the fact that all the books came from God. I now realize that many of the books are altered, and I reach back to the last revelation for clarification. However, a teacher in

Islam told me, "Islam is your gold, your dollar. The other spiritual books are like your silver, change, quarters. Do you throw away your silver, your change, your quarters just because you now have gold?"

That short allegory would take years to dissect. But as I grew spiritually, it would explain the void I carried within my religious belief. I will never claim to be where I desire to be with God, but I will also not let the shaitan trick me into believing that a change has not occurred. It is true; I will never be the same. The little girl I once knew is all grown up now. She knows the Grim Reaper is real. He still haunts her dreams and raids her relationships with family and people I tend to love. But most definitely, my friend list is short.

Chapter Twenty-Two
Children

MY GREATEST TEST and trial have been my children. Trying to balance the abuse and the hatred but remain pure of heart when it comes to them has been difficult. I spent my life protecting them from what I felt was my fate, putting them first financially, thinking about their future when I had not even begun to assess my own. I recall fighting with my family to save my children from the opinions they held. I remember my youngest daughter lying to get what she wanted without ever understanding the consequences of her words. CPS has grown to be a crock of bullshit in many cases. They seem to lose more white children to death at the hands of their parents than blacks. It is a cultural difference whether the world accepts it or not. I faced laws that are just filings. My daughter loved to run away and stay in the street because she liked gang banging and videotaping herself fighting. She needed the abuse to feel something because of our separation due to prison.

I would chase her and have the police tell me it is a thirteen-year-old child's right to refuse to be housed. They let these children walk around the streets of Minnesota, set them on display for abuse. They have no system in place to deal with this epidemic. Black children are falling through the cracks. Most parents give up. I fought until I had my daughter safely off those wicked streets where children were dying. Young girls being prostituted; not all because their parents were abusive. Many parents work like I did. The children want to be grown, so society gave them a don't-mind-your-parent card. CPS. I had my car windshield kicked and cracked in front of the police by my child, and they assumed that nothing was wrong. But if they try to restrain her and she throws a fit, then they want to charge the child with assault. When the courts intervene and take the control from parents who try to raise their children to not indulge in street violence, it was a fight here Minnesota. But when a police officer harms a youth, the world is sitting here ramping and raging about what happened. Look back to the source. Had they let parents raise their children, the police would not have to be beating them and stealing their lives. It is another way to help incite a genocide. I will always love my children more than I can ever begin to compare my love to. But I will not accept any abuse from their tempers and rage. Abuse is abuse.

I did a little different from a lot of parents with no answers. I went to court and petitioned it. Petition I filed was "I can afford to take care of my child; however, she is in need of protection from herself." She will not let me clothe and feed her. She is without food, medical, and housing when she is on the run. She had been a victim of sexual predators although she thought she was willing. There is no willingness between girls twelve to sixteen and guys eighteen to thirty. These babies still do not know good personal hygiene yet. I am still reminding my child to brush her teeth. After three years of fighting in Minnesota, I finally found a couple of judges who believed that a child's life matters whether we were in a Black community or not.

That is when God began to teach me again about prejudice. Since my child had fallen through the cracks, no matter how many times I sought professional and legal help to save her, I began to quit believing in justice. My sister had just buried my nephew. Many other Black victims were on the news. That is when I decided on what I could have done to help with the epidemic of lost children in this world. I had to make an impact on myself. I finally spoke to an officer, and he began to help me try and find a way to save my child. I discovered that there were female officers trying to pick those little girls up and get them off the streets. I was not the only one sick with outrage. Circumstances separate groups of people. It is when we began to change the way we think about situations that we may find answers. There will be some shitty and lazy officers. But there will always be some that stand behind what is right and just. We just have to decide on what that is. The fact that we need body cams, the fact that we are paying out lawsuits for wrongful death, and the fact that we must retrain mean that there has always been something that has been broken. How much damage has already been done? And what will it take for Black Americans to begin to heal?

Chapter Twenty-Three

Truth

I HAVE COME TO accept that I will have no healing until I accept my truth. The truth stands in facts. I am bruised deeply. My mother's heart was bruised deeply. I am subtracting the broken people my mother and I encountered, through our revelations from God. Unfortunately, spiritualists have a Bible, many the Quran, and some the Torah. Why? Because these are history books, full of time and scriptures to allow us to know we were not alone. Justice is the foundation of righteousness. From every righteous intervention, there was once spoken of a transgression. The world does not want to break scripture down for man to understand, quoting scriptures and not accepting the simple transgression going on in the home. So, my mother's teachers were broken. God gave them the law, and religion was the fabrication of man. So, this truth has kept me and my mother on an endless hope for the creator when he was there inside our heart had we just opened.

Now history has repeated itself again; on May 7, 2021, my eighteen-year-old daughter overdosed on promethazine and fentanyl. Death has reintroduced himself to me. As I sat in my home preparing for Mother's Day, a police card from the city of Minneapolis was left in my mailbox. A neighbor informed me. As I read that card, it said please contact Chicago Police. I immediately knew it was trouble, and something was wrong with my daughter. I told my oldest daughter. We had been calling her phone and received no answer. I called my family to come to the house as I made that call. I received the news I spent six years trying to avoid. They were looking for the next of kin. I could only scream in agony. An emotion I had not felt in a long time took over. That hidden woman began to surface. I was numb. I needed answers, and I was going to get them. As we were planning to get on the highway, a number was left for me.

It was the guy who was tricking young girls into stripping and illicit acts for money. He wanted to explain he did not call the police because he had a warrant. He initially said he found her body cold as ice. I would learn that this was a lie. He allowed her to slip away. She received no CPR. He told me I could get her phone and pick up her belongings. I got in my car, and within forty-five minutes, I was packed and headed to Chicago, the place I had left so many years ago, a place I never raised any of my children in. I was now heading back here. Driving in contemplation on how this meet would go, I reached out to the GDs and alerted them I was on my way. My baby died in an apartment on Carpenter. I needed aid and assistance. After twenty-five years, it was still there. We hit the city, and I waited for the appointed time to meet this mystery man she kept hiding. I was still numb. I could not even cry anymore.

As Tone met us there and let me in the apartment and I

walked in the room where she died, it was cold. It was lonely; what would have made her choose this is the question. As I kneeled to the floor to touch my baby's fluids, I looked up at this man's face. We were about twenty deep and were not coming in peace if it came to that. As he gave me the cell phone, he had wiped clean, he looked at me and said to let him know if I needed anything. In my hurt, I wanted to say, "I need you, bro, an eye for an eye." But I finally gave a motion for everyone to exit. After the change in my life, I did not want to be responsible for the deaths of so many if a shoot-out had occurred. After visiting the police station, we headed back to Minnesota to lay Star to rest.

I had to pull it together and decide on her funeral arrangements and lay her down as a Muslim in her last moments atop of the dirt, knowing that the grave was cold. She was under *Shahada* but was not practicing. I had not been the greatest example in those last couple of years. It was in my silence that I was leaning once again to Allah for directions. We were not strained for funds, so we needed a GoFundMe page, and I thank Allah for that. I would not have been able to stomach much more for fear I would have lost it. My oldest daughter said, "Mom, I have five thousand," but I answered, "No, baby." To many of the families' surprises, I had insurance. I hesitated to be not learned about the significance of having it. After being encouraged to do so by an insurance agent, I was buying it for myself because I assumed I would go first. Her policy came about as a whole life; it was to be a savings that I would leave her for when she got it together. That day just never came. As I tried to make peace with any decision Allah has allowed, we buried Star on Thursday. No sooner than we laid her to rest, I got the news about the gentleman we met who let her die and never called the police. Twenty-two warrants for his arrest had crashed his car, and he died that morning.

I was not overjoyed, nor was I saddened. It is as Allah has allowed it to be. I share this portion of my life as a reminder for abused women that we have options. As a struggling Muslim parent, death does not always miss our children. Educate them and give them the tools they need to survive. Like the famous words once spoken. Gangs are like social clubs for the ghetto. The will always exists. Instruct your child about life. Some things we cannot hide or shield. Prepare them for life because life prepares for them.

This battle I faced continuously trying to guide my daughter on a different path from the one I had taken had already began to take its toll on me spiritually and mentally.

I cannot help but think if I had not allowed the system to help me with the Caucasian methodology, my daughter would still be here. It is in my opinion that systems are put in place for African American families to create discord in the homes and destroy the family bonds, the need to execute social separation and identify the empowerment of other ethnic groups, which breaks the spirit of the African American. In treatment under the direct supervision of CPS, my daughter was slammed up against a wall. She phoned me and alerted me right away. I alerted the courts. The question came up, but no sanctions were ever given. We wonder why our African American adolescents get released from treatment and spiral right back under control. They build up resentment from their experience, and we lose them further and further into the system. This is what I had done. In an attempt to stop her fate from being like mine, I set the stage. Unknowingly, I had allowed the system to break Star's will. When I began to speak on it, not one social worker ever returned my call. Not one even showed up for her burial. In life, they were always showing up trying to get her to allow herself to be adopted. I even got a paper in my mail calling me a foster parent. This was how messed up their files were. Star would alert me every time. She might have wanted to live life on her on terms but separate herself from me never. She was intelligent enough to never accept that offer. In those moments, she was stronger than I.

Chapter Twenty-Four
Young John

I OFTEN WONDER WHERE John is now. It was John who gave me the function of uniting the SOS women together. He had given a nineteen-year-old that much power without explaining everything it entailed. I was young. I had not developed mentally to be able make an educated decision about my life. He gave me a privilege and a curse that I did not understand how to control. Watching people perish in the streets became normal. I accepted it. I had no idea that my loyalty would cost me everything I had ever known.

Loyalty is a mechanism that is used to solidify courage, partnerships, bonds, and relationships. Be careful to whom you offer your loyalty. Know where your loyalty begins and ends.

In my severe misconception of loyalty, I assumed that protecting a foundation no matter what it was built on was required. Even after a shooter gunned us and the car down on November 28, 1991, I never ever showed up in court against my attackers. After learning I had been ambushed by our own people, I still never processed that deceit until recently, almost a quarter of a century later. Lil Frank said, "Magic, you were not supposed to be in that car." Process that for a second. I was a gangster with morals. Women, children, and the elderly were always off limits when the scales weighed in on elevated levels. I had taken my six-year-old son out of the car just hours before that horrific incident occurred. I valued loyalty, and it was betrayed. I learned loyalty from young John.

John came home with a vision that he had learned from the ole man himself. It was a light so bright that one needed to taste the nectar to harvest it. For many of the GDs like me, we lacked that opportunity.

Some of us came from parents with incredibly low-paying wages or no jobs at all, not to mention having parents struggling with drug addictions. Fighting this low status in life, some could not see what King David had intended. We missed the reminders from Hoover. It is in his brief lapse in judgement as a young man that his whole life has been stolen. Circumstances have locked away and trapped seasons and reoccurring seasons of knowledge that can benefit the world in a Colorado prison.

It is because of Hoover that I can accept the discipline I need to establish my daily prayers in Islam. Allah has allowed me to cross a path so that I can understand that he is the supreme being, and no one deserves the right to be praised but Allah SWT and him alone. Young John handed me that power, but Hoover's vison allowed me the ability to think beyond the ghettos of this world. In my days of Jalal eel, the Gangster Disciples' organizational teachings did not fail me. Some of its people did. I failed to live according to the teachings I was reading and became intertwined with the way individuals chose to lead. In my younger years, I failed to see past the corruption that seeped into the streets. I failed to be a part of the change. I got caught up within the brutality of gang life and not organizational structure. Larry Hoover cannot be blamed for that. I must accept responsibility for my own actions. No man can bear another man's burdens. I will not downplay the loss of life in the world—we read it every day—nor will I ever downplay the generosity of Larry Hoover. I was encouraged with fatherly advice to think about a career and secure a place in life before I became a single mom with many children. Since we knew not the principles of Islam in our days, that was the soundest advice anyone could have given me.

I did not fully understand what Hoover meant. He was speaking on financial stability. A concept I was not familiar with. I will always be grateful for Mr. Hoover for allowing me a chance to have a choice. I had caught a couple drug cases while being on Slick Payroll, and he was cruddy. He was not helping us young folks pay for lawyers. It is when I met Ted and Mac here and became a part of 21st Century VOTE that I truly came to learn about the structure in more depth. With there being so many folks, I know individuals I have come in contact with such as W. who did not remember sending me one hundred dollars on Christmas in prison. I do though.

She really did not remember much about our relationship. She had suffered a stroke over the years. Nonetheless, she had paid for the lawyer for me. They tried to keep me out of prison on cases that had nothing to do with their relationship with me. So, for this, I will always be grateful.

I was told to be in the political arena, I could not pedal any narcotics. It was forbidden. Had I stayed on that course the rest of my life, I never would have saw federal prison. When you never learn from the first lesson, it just repeats itself. I learned that lesson many years later. I had already paid the price by watching many of my loved ones die in the world. These were things young John could not control, because by now, he no longer existed in my life.

Chapter Twenty-Five
Shorty G

AFTER REMINISCING, I also have been contemplating about the dangers John had put me in with him, ushering me into that position in the organization. The dangerousness of being bestowed functions and power can hold life and death in one's hands. I had been introduced to this function with no title. As people began to describe me with the titles, they deemed appropriate, it almost set me up for a fatal encounter.

I was on the East Side representing GD. I had been introduced to Jimmy D, so he knew who I was and that I was legit. However, no one informed Shorty G of who I was. As my name and popularity began to surface, Shorty sent them goons to scoop me up and bring me to him in Avalon Park. To falsely claim to be a GD or have a function could get you hospitalized or worse in those days. As the cars arrived, Jimmy D rode with me to the park. When I arrived at the park, I saw a group of women. They were SOS. That immediately heightened my senses to know they were there for me. The sisters were there to stomp my brains out had any information came back unconfirmed.

After what seemed like an eternity on cell phones and pagers, my status within the organization was now verified. The legendary Shorty G had stamped the approval. The investigation into my strange identity was now concluded. Again, I had been waiting in the lion's den. I was allowed to speak to the sisters that day from Shorty's area, which was very enlightening. I made one key mistake that day. I did not align myself with the East Side. I would have then had that umbrella of a board member in my corner, which I came to know later is sometimes needed. Again, it is a privilege and a curse if you make any mistakes.

Shorty G became a significant factor in my life. It was always him I turned to in my times of trouble, like when we beat a brother with bottles, sticks, and bats. They complained on my actions as a female, suggesting we should be of the powerless. My reasoning was sound. A male member of our organization disrespected us. Status and reputation were everything. If he, does it, the opposition will too. So, like the female bosses we were, we tore a lining in the brother that day. Blood was everywhere. This was required to obtain that level of respect we were achieving in those days.

It was Boo's area, and we were at odds currently in my life. We had an unpleasant history. I had fumbled a front of two ounces of cocaine, something a young woman such as myself should have never encountered. He gave it to me, and someone close to me ran off with a portion, and the other portion I had caught a drug charge on. That was street life in Englewood. So, Boo stayed mad with me for years behind that mistake. So, yes, I needed a board member in my corner.

Shorty was charismatic, and I fell in love with a young man under his teachings. Lil Frank. Frank was young like me, unlearned and unaware of the territory we had trailed as young adults. The sacrifices we would have to make. The sacrifices that many before us have made. The cat in the hat. True to his name and nature in every sense of the word. It was Shorty who knew I stood by my beliefs, and I would prove loyal when many of the brothers would not. Knowing what could be discussed and what one will take to the grave. Still standing on that now. This book is to paint a picture of how dangerous street life can be for the youth. To acknowledge Allah SWT power and mercy even when I knew him not.

I do not think I ever really believed in the devil in those days. I have learned since then that he believed in me.

He was constantly trying to take my life, and I can only imagine Allah SWT saying not yet. Not right now. She has unfinished business.

If you ask me how I feel about how many of our leaders' fates has ended up, I will tell you; for me, I believe in mercy past any mistakes now. I am always praying to Allah for forgiveness. How can I only want that forgiveness for myself? The conspiracies I have read about many of their cases, I cannot fully agree with. Other than that close encounter in Avalon Park, I never saw any hostile parts of Shorty. He always remained calm, even when his brother passed. I came to the funeral because I wanted to show my respect to Shorty. I know no matter what goes on in lives, family is family. So, seeing Shorty contain his hurt and anger, I just see him in a different light. He is now serving a life sentence for that huge GD conspiracy that incarcerated so many men of stature. I only know him to be true to his belief. Anything else that does not concern me I leave alone.

Chapter Twenty Six
The Fight

AT THE DAWN of a new day, I began to create new ideas. My inner self became color-blind as I looked out toward humanity. The separations I had created in my anger against maltreatment and prejudice of the Chicago Police Department have soon faded. They are humans with flaws just like me. They just sit in positions that sometimes-spread havoc in communities. There will always be a good police officer and a bad cop. That is the balance whether the world perceives it not. I built my foundation on the trust none suspect all as my basis, and for what it is worth, it is solid. However, there are some variations in your struggle. Instead of identifying a select group for the identification to the maltreatment I had endured during my life, such as lack of opportunity to better schooling, affordable housing for my mom, connection to spirituality, and mental health treatment and financial separation, my focus became to observe the system put in place to remove stumbling blocks, as my Imam brother Makram has taught me. I had to be a part of changing the narrative. What had I done for my own people, and what have I tried to change my own predicament?

My inner self has had one foot headed on the straight path while my latter food dangled in the *dunya*. My ability to cope and overcome carried a double-edged sword for me. Not yet fully submitting to the will of Allah SWT in every endeavor of my life was the true struggle that was a microcosm of everything that surrounded me. It is written that Allah SWT never changed the condition of people until they first change what is in their hearts. I muscled up all the strength I could find, and I headed to the masjid. Masjid An-Nur.

For quite some time, I had fallen back on my heels. I remained stagnated in my growth even though I possessed what many have not found. Guidance. I had begun to follow the easier path despite the restlessness. For those actions, heavy was the cost I had to pay. My children fell by the wayside all around me. I was being tested during my disobedience to Allah SWT. I had responsibilities as a parent to hold on tight to the rope of Allah SWT with no excuse to loosen the grip. I was again human falling to the lower parts of my *nafs*.

The cultivation of my Eman was so painful as I turned back to the straight path. Losing Star was my ultimate challenge. Then came the test of my youngest son throwing his life away despite all I had been through. He had witnessed it all for himself. Any advice had fallen on death ears, even the advice from two reconciliating sides, his father and me. For years, we blamed each other for what should have been and for what should not have ever occurred. I was now able to find peace for the war we had waged against each other over our son.

The more peace was restored, the more my son strayed. He was no longer able to pit the parenting skills of his parents against each other. Once the harmony was restored between me and big client, my hands were clean within my journey to make amends with seasons in my life. I now drew a line between relationships that I would allow to live rent free in my spirit.

Chapter Twenty-Seven

Mrs. Mary

WITH EACH NEW day and the power of Allah SWT to touch so many, I am discovering peace. For years, I assumed I had no taste for Mary. Ms. Mary, as she is called, would prove to be better than our initial meeting. By circumstances, we were enemies for years. By Allah, we would come to hold mutual respect and the love that God requires us to hold for humanity.

I met my first husband when I was twenty-three years old and six months pregnant after that terrible shooting that G Sharp lost his life in. As the survivor of that tragedy, it left me with a child who would never know a father figure. That would have been better for me if I only knew better. Instead, I met CD. He would frequently visit, and he gained the family stamp of approval. Everyone knew what I needed more than me. This is that Christian side of the family that believes it is better to marry than not burn in hell. Marriage is always honorable. However, it will always have its time and season. This was not my season. CD was in a long-term five-year relationship with a woman almost twenty years his senior. His family did not approve. This is where the chaos begins. As I try and put the circumstances I was in into focus, the devil came from so many directions. In Islam, I would have had to wait at least six months after death to even try and be on a clear path to being able to articulate the profound changes in my life.

Instead of the elders in my family and his pushing to do what was morally right, they pushed us toward marriage. I was already so young and wild from the street life and still tied to the GD organization within my heart and in everything I knew. Sadly, the organization would undergo a federal indictment. Members I knew and communicated with were being picked up. One of the topics that would become known was the shooting I endured. Avoiding the trouble back home, I settled into that marriage, allowing CD to abandon Ms. Mary and start a new life with me. The tragedy was I never stay in relationships long at all. That was that abuse mechanism that I suffered.

There were no forms or trust that can be established when your every guard is up. Then the encounter with me and Ms. Mary happened. As my daughter was born, I started to realize I was in a marriage that I never wanted, and lives were being destroyed. As we would separate and make up, were involving individuals in the chaos. On a particular day, as Ms. Mary was driving my husband's car and we were being sued for the payment on a loan we took against the car, I immediately approached as she exited. I jumped in the car to pull off within, and his elderly parents were in that car. My cousin was too afraid to move my car, screaming we were going to get in trouble with the police. I got back out of the car. As I got in my vehicle, she hurried and pulled off with her family. I followed and I ran my vehicle into the back of my husband's car. Not too hard, just enough to make my point. Immediately, my husband sent his brother to retrieve the car from her. As I drove around searching for the car after the first incident, my husband's brother was driving, and I went about my normal day. If she was not driving, I would have been satisfied.

Days would pass, and I would soon discover she had an adult daughter as old as I was. She was heavyset in weight, and I barely was 125 pounds. She approached me and jammed me up in a corner with three other heavy women. They were big. As she questioned me about what happened, in my defensive voice, I said, "Fuck your mama," and I jumped in my car and tried to run them over. The gentlemen I was seeing intervened and prevented the action. However, he was the reason they found where I stayed. He worked with Mary's daughter and fed her all the information she needed. That betrayal.

As he went and decided he was going to hang out with them and had me drop him off at a residence, The daughter was there. There was a huge exchange of words, and it was now on. I went and grabbed a cousin, went back to fight, but realized my cousin was not up for that challenge that day. These were some big women. So, I went and grabbed a friend who I know was not afraid to get down. Esha's reputation did not supersede her. She was that one. As we pulled back up, I had a bat and a hunting dagger that has always been on my door's side. I got out of the car and told her to bring it. She saw Aisha and charged me with a knife. I grabbed the bat and just started beating her with it. The knife was unable to reach me, so she threw it and charged me. Now we are hand fighting, and her weight pulls us both to the ground. As I kept punching her from the angle, I was positioned on the ground, and one of her friends moved to break it up. Fight was in my favor, so immediately, Aisha grabbed the knife and just began to stab and cut. In like a minute, blood was everywhere, and we just looked at each other. It was Mother's Day. In my anger, the only thing I could say was, "Tell your mama happy Mother's Day." Her friends no longer helped her. They put our knife back in our car for us. We took it and tossed it in the river, knowing the police were coming, after pressing charges for her charging me with the knife first. I looked at my friend who was on probation, and I told her I would take this loss. I would plead guilty.

As Mary's daughter pressed charges, as I knew she would, I turned myself in, pleaded guilty to the stabbing, and posted bond. By a fluke of blessings, Ms. Mary's daughter agreed that I stabbed her. Never mentioned there was a bat, so I was charged with aggravated assault with a deadly weapon. A knife. Two years later, as the trial came, my case would get tossed out. This whole time trying to protect Aisha, the jail held her anyway until court. When the truth came out and Aisha made a deal with probation to extend it for her actions, the case was tossed out to me. I had been charged with the wrong count, and that charge could not be reissued to the correct one. I did not know it then, but that error would change my life indefinitely. I now work for so many jobs that a violent offense would have been prevented. I will always be apologetic for all the lives that got destroyed that day. A friendship separated by circumstances. I did see Aisha the day of trial, and she thanked me for taking the rap. She said her lawyer explained what I had done for her. The police holding her was of their own will. She told me to go in there and beat my case. She pleaded guilty. That would be the last time I would see my friend because I moved over four hours away. But she will never be forgotten.

Neither will Ms. Mary. After all that chaos, Ms. Mary would find forgiveness to help my ex-husband raise my two children as I went to federal prison sometime later on a narcotics charge. My ex-husband, despite my daughter not being his blood but carrying his name, would take custody of the children until my release. Many mistakes were made over the years I was away. There is no blame today. I allowed the circumstances that would lead me to prison to occur. It was Allah's intervention that led me to Islam. It was these tragedies that allowed my eyes to open and my ears to hear. There were so many Islamic lessons in this brief encounter. We just must learn from them. Without my journey away from all things in my grasp, I would never have been able to appreciate the opportunities I have always had. I spent my life looking for the reason why I did not advance from that lowly place I had known for so long. I was my own worst enemy. The world was never supposed to make me complete.

I needed to discover that completion for myself. Islam was the 360-degree circle we spoke of reaching as GD...s. I just had not tapped into the mercy of Allah SWT. I had not found my intimate place with the creator. A place where I relinquish all my weakness to, Allah and Allah alone. In my ignorance, I looked for it in people.

Chapter Twenty-Eight

Gangs

BECOMING A GD at eighteen years of age had not quite allowed me to develop an adult thinking process within the limited exposure of my subconscious. At eighteen years old, I had only seen Englewood, the South Side of Chicago, Mississippi where I am a native of, and Downtown Chicago, Jones Commercial High School, the school I attended briefly in my junior year. Again, those famous words often spoken by Mr. Hoover, "Gangs are the social clubs of the ghetto." The separated class of people labeled through the separation between the fortunate, the less fortunate, and those bound by areas in life that lacked less or no exposure to creativity. Things that you discover as an adult in African American history but was hidden from the grasps of lower- and middle-class people during the years of our development. The years that reared us into the young men and women we were striving to be. In our righteous endeavors to become better humanitarians and position ourselves financially toward a better economic status, we became a group of men and women with negative labels before we even had a chance to establish the productivity that we were being taught to usher in.

As the title *gang* is circulated, we become less than other organizations, such as country clubs and well-to-do nonprofits that create jobs and opportunities for themselves. Here in Minnesota, I have worked for a few country clubs, with wealthier classes of people paying twenty thousand dollars for a membership fee.

Waiting on list to do so. With many African American families and Latinos, that is a year's wage, if not less. As GDs tried to position themselves toward a better economic future, we were blocked politically, culturally, economically, and socially. Targets were placed on our backs. We were ravaged by systems claiming to have Americans' best interest at heart when they were igniting the fires that was forcing people to survive the only way they had been introduced to.

I remember meeting a young lady dating BM Speedy, whom I do not know personally. She and her sister, who also dated another BM, were creating GD watches and apparel. This would seem to an entrepreneur a great investment. It was productive. No different from many other brand names that existed. However, production was blocked. The government has held many African American people back from creating righteous opportunities for themselves and others, organizational structures that seem not to fit into America's norm for society.

When you are not allowed to manufacture goods for wholesale even when following protocol just as the rest of society, this discriminatory move devours human hope, buries self-esteem, and keeps trapped in a barrel with others fighting to break free or just move to the top like the rest of the world. How did the government expect positivity when they threw the people crumbs and expect us to accept the hypocrisy the world was offering us? We were just trying to break free from the oppression done in Jim Crow's days, still battling ethnic separations as well as many people just discovering what same-sex relationships entailed and how it was perceived in society. We were battling territories we were not equipped to manage at that moment. We had no psychologist and no counselors, and I do not ever remember having a social worker growing up in school. We were separated from the world. So, an opportunity to be a part of something great was a poor person's dream.

My writings will never capture the culture of street gangs because my words will never do justice in an explanation to honor the loss and the achievements that certain organizational structures have endured over the course of half a century. There will always be good and evil in everything we encounter. If you go to dinner and constantly overeat, you are labeled a glutton; if you commit adultery, you are in a world of sinful behavior. If you remove something that does not belong to you, you have stolen. If you lie like so many police officers do to incarcerate the alleged bad guys, that is a sin. However, many say it is for the greater good. But for who's good? For the officer who made lieutenant lie. For the community that allowed an individual to be wrongfully sentenced.

Black on Black crimes, I am not disputing that crime exists.

I am only clarifying that the privilege to do harm to any individual is wrong. We either are trusting systems set in place even if it is not harsh enough in one's opinion.

I have seen so many tragic losses in life. I pray to be delicate with my words because families have endured so much from death's kiss that I dare not underplay its causes and effects. With me being raised in Chicago, my path crossed many. I respected other organizational beliefs even when they differed from mine. They were all needed at contrasting times to open the minds of people. How they were used by some became the problem. I remember meeting Shorty Freeman. It was during the peace treaty GDs and BDs had in place. He was on house arrest when Ted and I visited him. Ted delivered the intended message, which was about politics, voting, and standing firm to curve some of the gun violence that was happening in the streets. We were a part of 21st Century VOTE, and it had a special meaning to so many people who wanted change. Trying to unite the Black brothers and sisters to make them politically aware of their surroundings and the chainages that were affecting the black neighborhoods was on the agenda. That was my first only meeting with Shorty Freeman. He was very hospitable and appeared to be an upright person who wanted something different for his people as well. It had to have been for us to be in a sit-down. I choose to remember the positivity I saw on that day.

I would later come to meet and love another BD brother, BD Zeb from what was known as the Calumet Building back then in the '90s. A real smart-ass and a true gentleman of the ghetto. He looked past circumstances and tried to fight for what he wanted through any means necessary. He clowned me at first. My clothing. I had been on house arrest for a spell, and the clothes I wore had played its name out. I had just come off, and I had to wear something. There were no finances coming in while I was on that pending case.

After mocking me, a stranger to him, meeting at a friend's house as she was scoring her package of cocaine, we were verbally at odds. I was pissed. I was a female though. Had I been a male, we would have ended in blows. As I exited and went to my court date that day, I later returned with my young son named Dollar Bill, often spoiled in his childhood by many of the GD..s. As I arrived with Bill, and he was playing, that foul-mouthed man returned with what Sharon needed. Upon his return, he saw my handsome young son who was dressed to impress. My clothes may have missed a date but not my son's. Jordans, towel coats, and designer jeans by damage. It was popular at that time. He asked Sharon whose son was that, and she told him, "That's Magic's son, the dusty girl." I was hot as hell. But it did not matter. That was my financial condition at that time.

BD Zeb had a reputation for being a good man to the women he dated. After seeing my son well taken care of, it sparked an interest in me. He wanted a date, and I was like hell no. But he made an offer a young girl could not refuse. He wanted to take me and my son to dinner. If I went, he would take me shopping as well. So, I humbly obliged. We went to Red Lobster, which was foreign to me. I had not traveled much out of Englewood yet. Dinner was amazing because I had his full attention. No disrespect, just kindness.

He still wanted to know how a person who held a title with the GDs was dressing so low-grade. I defended my belief and just answered it is not about the money but the vision. As promised, he took me shopping; and when he shops for a woman, he completes an outfit, from shoes, to underwear, to socks, to clothes to the hairdo. In the time spent together in each other's life, I never wanted anything. I had ounces of cocaine, and every dime made was mine. I spent it as I saw fit. But like the story of my life, nothing lasts for me. I became pregnant. I was taking my prenatal as prescribed by a doctor. Life was good except he needed full control, and that was something I could not relinquish. I was a GD, and that was that. I later learned that GDs had murdered his brother, so amazingly, I could understand that hatred. I just never knew the position I was in. It's complicated to love someone who represents differently. Even in Islam, it says believing men are for believing women. We are to marry our own kind, not from other religions. With this being such a separatism and he tells you when you can leave the house, it did become a problem later. During that time, my menstruation fell, so

I assumed I miscarried. He was angry, so we separated. Later the next month, I was still with child. It was a brief spotting. Since we had gone our separate ways, in my ignorance, I did what I thought was best, and I did not bring that child in this world. Lifelong regrets now that I have lost my daughter. Always wondering what life could have been like if I had followed through with bringing that new life into this world.

I am not against a woman doing what she thinks is best for herself. However, for me, I am left with a lifetime of regrets. I now cherish all life so deeply. I had no right to abort. Not being religious in those days, I acted the only way I knew how to. Inshallah, I pray that Allah has granted me mercy from taking life.

Chapter Twenty-Nine
The Sacrifice

I CAN FIND NEITHER peace within chaos nor redemption through apologies. It is only in physically elevating the world where I have released havoc can I truly find peace.

Becoming a part of anything in life requires some sacrifice. The million-dollar question is what you are willing to sacrifice. For Mr. Hoover, I believe his sacrifice may have been greater than any I have seen in the normality of what I call my walk-in life. Mr. Hoover has sacrificed freedom, family, and self-gratification.

He may almost appear to have a sealed fate. In my walk among the Gangster Disciples, many sacrifices were made. The sacrifice became evident as you consumed the blueprints, the written history books we lived by. Many people like Shorty Bible; TJ, now known as Ayyub; and Young John so eloquently faded out in silence. These men of stature, in their times studied fervently, as one may call it. They believed in a vision that held so much merit to an African American community that needed hope in the '80s and '90s. We needed a dream to evolve. The barrier that stood between our excellence was finances and loyalty. The individuals we encountered on so many levels believed in personal gain, exploiting the people and the vision. This is what has created Mr. Hoover's sacrifice. He has had to hold the weight of every mistake made by generations over time of more than fifty years.

The world, the government, and the people all need someone to blame when the situation supersedes their control. The world we live in is operated by control. Whoever sits in the driver's seat is always responsible, whether physically present or not. I will not sit here and convey that life within the organizational structure was pleasant for me because it was not. It was the sacrifice I chose to make, and it was a heavy penalty to pay. I had my image tainted on so many occasions. Inside my subconscious, I believed I was in control. A young lady given the power to unite a sisterhood and bring the masses together. I was one of many chosen in my time. I was given status at the wrong time in my life. I was too young to understand, too naive to comprehend the dangers and too passive to undertake the sacrifice. I was just living in someone else's dream. I had not found a dream of my own. Integrating myself within this period has now helped me define my own self-worth, helped me discover that I am a fighter. I have always possessed the capabilities of touching the lives of others. I just needed to discover my strengths and weaknesses, accept my mistakes and failures, and use them as steppingstones for more innovative ways to touch a nation of my people.

I see the Black and brown brothers and sisters struggling every day to bring about change economically, spiritually, physically, and mentally. This has become self-evident because of the lessons I have learned as a former member of the Gangster Disciples. My mistakes I hold as my own; my pain I elevate and rise far beyond its reach. I have chosen to move forward in faith and not linger behind in the past. My sacrifice is now my own. I take from the past the good, the misinterpreted information, and I consume it for what it is. What it was once meant to be. I am a replica today of what could have existed yesterday had the governing forces properly guided us that we served. There remains a sense of loyalty to a few. Not many. Time has proved the faithful few within my circle.

We stand today in solidarity with each other. Each on their own path, religious beliefs, and careers.

However, what we hold in common is where we came from in those trenches in the streets—the pain we endured, the losses we have grown to accept, and the strength we have gained within our connections to our spirituality. This is what we hold on too, not the lies we believed but the misguided information. That solidifies that the information was just delivered incorrectly and executed poorly by some. This caused many to sacrifice their freedoms, their families, and their dreams. I am sympathetic to the loss of some soldiers to the penal system. I am overwhelmed by the deaths of my brothers and sisters who have preceded me and the loss of my eighteen-year-old daughter who was fascinated by a past that I chose to not completely share. I wonder if it would have changed her fate as it changed mine. These are the memories you carry as a burden and reminder of the work that is required in life. Therefore, I strive for excellence despite the barriers; this is the sacrifice. I have known many men in my life. Some would now attest that carrying the weight of the organization with any status requires sacrifice. I remember the first time I saw Frank as a free man again. He had come to Minnesota for whatever purpose on his agenda. He talked with my son. The little boy whom he took for a haircut was now a grown man. As he spoke to me about life lessons, I realized he had not fully accepted his. He would find himself in a dilemma requiring the sacrifice. Who's sacrifice I do not know. What I do know is after completing a twenty-year sentence and having an excellent job making good money, he is now back incarcerated. I ask myself; I wonder what he feels about the sacrifice he just made?

He just left his newborn precious sprout again. He had already missed seeing his other children grow up. He is now back in the same position. There can never be change holding on to the past. It is in the rear view of your life for a reason. To revisit it, I cannot understand. It is not my sacrifice to choose. It was his.

These are the sacrifices we make, the actions we partake in, a political choice. Once you have been incarcerated for lengthy periods of time, to even risk a mere thought of return is incomprehensible to me.

Some of us, I imagine, are still full of sacrifices. I have given all I have to man's ideology. I am striving to give my latter to Allah SWT.

The world in its greatest illusion needs someone to answer the mistakes it makes aimed at communities it has allowed to be oppressed. We politically wage the war on drugs, gun rights, human trafficking, exploitation of women, and the upliftment of indigenous lives; but have we created a true system of process that guarantees the victims or survivors will reap the proceeds accrued? The answer is simply no. A community member received the votes that they needed to be aligned in a position to create the change, but rarely does a change create enough difference in the lives of the people it mattered the most.

What will Indigenous people have to sacrifice to promote the change? We as a people are as guilty as many of the ex-offenders we prosecute. We allowed the stronger political influences to dictate the structure of a nation that already had its own culture. In doing this, we see war, alliances broken, betrayal, and the survival instinct that the beast in all of us can create. We see it excel into the world and destroys the hope and change many of us for whom are classified as indigenous fight.

As an ex-offender and a woman in long-term recovery, I have accepted the responsibility to create the change within my own life. Only then can I uplift and share within another's life the hope to change the narrative. The narrative as I currently perceive it to be is that our children are dying way too young; communities are pulling further away from each other. We can blame these effects on men who have once established their existence, such as Larry Hover aka Chief, Jeff Fort, Shorty G., and all the African American men who fell victim to the indictment that disassembled a group of individuals discovering the possibility of unification. The streets of Chicago that I grew up in changed because of the abrupt removal of social statuses. This does not say that a change was not needed or should have been in place. What I stand by in direct conflict will be the operation used to target a group of people.

My eighteen-year-old daughter Star was supposed to live and create a new generation where we failed in our own decisions to choose to abort the true teachings of growth and development. As once stated, to wage war on drugs, we would have simultaneously needed to wage war on the mental health crisis in the African American community. We had no preparation to fight a demon we never knew existed. A child does not wake up with an inclination to kill, steal, or destroy. Those mechanisms are produced over time. Time away from the proper mental health assessments after a tragedy, after abuse has occurred and went undetected. Time away from healthy social interventions by faces that they relate to.

The system put in place in the '80s and '90s and early 2000s was not equipped to handle the truth. We were still living in modern-day slavery with no reparations to allow us to achieve the change I know many of us wanted within the organization structure I was a part of. We could only dream of something greater but not identify what that greatness was or how it could change our communities because we were under political and social attacks. We lacked the finances to create our own jobs, we lacked true unification, and we suffered from separatism within our own selves. We had no one who we could truly trust in massive numbers. Within each side of the city and areas, there were self-alliances. This was never supposed to thrive within a group of people who stood on the same principles.

We lied to ourselves and each other. We sacrificed an ideology without even understanding what we were doing. The sacrifice is the repercussion of denied freedoms for individuals that may or may not have fully changed their thought process. Nonetheless, we have denied groups of men and women the second chance we solicit all within the state and Federal laws. I am extremely blessed that the second-chance law touched my life. However, I am deeply saddened that has not touched enough lives. The sacrifice for Mr. Hoover is denied hope. To pray every day for change and to be admonished repeatedly… Many of us would have lost the fight to keep creating change. Produce positivity for those less fortunate. He never gave up on his dream. It appears the dream had given up on His sacrifice. A sacrifice that had changed my life.

No one should ever have to carry that banner. Not even those who have made mistakes. God's Forgiveness supersedes all.

Chapter Thirty

Ethnic Trauma

WE ARE WEARY, we are tired. We were traumatized before our prison sentence ever expired. We rejoice now that we are told we are free. But I still witness the African American community overpopulated and confined by modern day slavery.

We were labeled as an enemy of the State.

My flaw was dreaming about tomorrow on time that was borrowed, the world did not comprehend until the end what they were doing to the African American women and children when they locked up and incarcerated our Black men.

On a genocidal level, they knew our offspring would become weakened with the father figure removed.

For my Sons I fight with all my might to teach him to become a Power to Be and not just exist and allow their minds to become trapped within life circumstances.

Reparations was a tradeoff for freedom that needs renewing every so many years. So yes, we hold on to our fears holding distrust for some legislators. The ancestors of many of the congressional leaders were once a part of the oppression my grandmother warned me about.

So, we are free until the new law ushers in with the statement there is no need to for rehabilitation, hit that group with conspiracy. They are more valuable incarcerated. We will work them for 12 cents to a 1.00 an hour manufacturing the goods and contracts the prisons take on. We will make market value for the labor. Prisons will get paid over 30,000 to house the inmates and thus jobs are created for your families. The new slave trade that is protected by fear and Histeria that the government made.

We found ourselves in these situations when crack cocaine hit the streets. We were oppressed and sought out as scape goats for the war on drugs. Now Crack cocaine versus meth and fentanyl.

Now we have discovered undiagnosed metal health which I know exists and drug rehab for a selected group of individuals has been created for treatment. New jobs were created while those who battled crack addictions still lay incarcerated because they were in pain at a different phase in time. So yes, African Americans are angry.

Alhamdulillah that Allah swt has allowed me to taste forgiveness and in return I know that I must offer it as well. So, in my heart I release peace and Mercy in my spirit.

In doing that I am so hurt that that Mercy is not extended to others. I ponder about Larry Hoover, Jeff Fort, Shorty G, and I wonder why mercy seems to fall on deaf ears. Sammy the Bull was released after being on a Case with Gaetti. Larry Hoover is still praying that someone will notice the change and dedication he has made to uplifting the youth and the African American community. Is man without flaw no. Have mistakes been made in life? yes. But at what part does forgiveness and rehabilitation become the driving force for change. Not being allowed to receive a letter or make a phone call outside of your family. Rights that other prisoners have. We pick and choose on laws. This is the oppression that almost kept me in bondage. Allah swt is the best of planners. I live to serv my community, the orphans and my elders. As traumatized as I was yesterday, With the mercy of Allah swt. I live in the Mercy of the Qadr of my life.

During my pain I discovered how my destiny was being fashioned in every instance of my life. Every choice I made had its own consequence.

Al Baqarah 286

My Lord does not place a burden on a soul more than it can bear.

So, I ponder how strong Larry Hoover must be mentally and how strong he is spiritually to have tried so often to share the best of himself while carrying so many other burdens.

Chapter Thirty-One
Loyalty Of A Queen

I NEEDED A ROLE model to compare my strengths and weaknesses to. I needed an example I could relate to. Winndye Hoover was one. Sue, as she is called, was another S2 bar and grill. Winndye has stayed loyal for almost two centuries praying that one day she will see change in her life of reunification of her complete family. It must be horrific Dealing with negative media. Even overwhelming positive media can bear its burden. Always trying to stay humble and awake to trying to find out how to usher change in to keep the ideology of someone You love moving forward. Walking in her own right as a first lady and living up to the task. Trying to help those of us who Love the Ole man as much as she can. I remember when I had briefly given up. Circumstances were overwhelming. I came back to Chicago and just walked away from my house. I was trying so hard to produce change and it appeared to fall on death ears. During my walk about I needed employment. She is called Ms. Sue as many call her. Sue and Scony gave me a job. They could not pay me what I was used to. But they paid me enough money to find time to decide my next move. Growth and Development, aid and assistance. No questions asked. I had gainful employment. I told Sue I was writing a book. I expounded about my life, and she was a listening ear. As a few weeks went by I accepted the fact I had to come back to Minnesota and go back to work and save my house. I had worked to hard for it. Ms. Sue Loyalty to her significant other and the community helped me figure out my next step in life. The Loyalty of a woman is something fierce. I stayed with Winndye until I could strengthen my wings and fly again. It is an awful burden for parents to watch their children suffering from bad choices and not be able to advise. I was reaching the world. However, I was failing with some of my offspring. As an example, from Winndye you just keep trying no matter what it takes to share the appropriate teachings needed at that time. So, if you're ever in Chicago and you really want to uplift the community. Reach out to those making sacrifices. Those who are watching people they love make sacrifices. If you have not lost someone to certain tragedies, you will never understand the depth of that love. Not because you are not open. But simply because you have not experienced loss.

Chapter Thirty-Two
Aid and Assistance

COMING UP TO Chicago there was so much aid and assistance as we fellowshipped together for positivity and Change. I never once went hungry or without shelter during my travel. Lexus Rob who owns Harold's Chicken on 87th off East End made sure I was safe and comfortable as I partook in a fabulous meal prepared for me as we broke bread as family. Allah swt is always the best of planners. In his Mercy he allowed brothers in my path to assist me in my righteous endeavor as I share our struggles and triumphs in life. We truly have grown and developed into a strong group of people who only desire is to serv God and the community. We first have to be true to ourselves, then each other. When a group of people change their hearts that is when Allah swt can further assist us in our development as a strong group of people.

Like Mrs. Winndye Hoover said "everyday life is a challenging adventure. We must take it one day at a time. We must stay focused and make good choices. Failure is not an option. These words hold true to those striving to do better in life. Refusing to accept the defeats we have face as African Americans fighting for a place and an opportunity to share and teach. It is my opinion that Mr. Hoover can offer more to the community than he had been given credit for. To understand a struggle, one must first have survived one. I watch wrappers who have felony convictions get caught with firearms. Money buys you freedom when the rest of the brothers and sisters of lesser statuses get penitentiary. When the laws start to be bi-partisan and we cannot come together for the greater good of humanity on the laws that adversely affect African Americans, or senior citizens, and our youth. My generation is still an endangered species. I will always respect Mr. Hoover. He will always be like a father to me as he has been for so many others in need of hope and guidance. I pray that Larry Hoover can find some peace and mercy from the Judges. 50 plus years is way too long for a person who eagerly tries to change the mindset of those who have lost their way.

He is not being held in my opinion because he is a danger to the community. He is being held because he has the intelligence to guide one to political awareness. He is feared because he can awaken the mindset of people who need someone, they can relate to in order to take their place in the political arena. Man, fears what he cannot control. Mr. Hoover is a man who can dream regardless of the oppression he has dealt with most of his life. Being Strong is his only charge. Mr. Hoover has not given up on anything in life. How many of us can say that? Jeff Fort fought for what he believed in despite the obstacles. If a man doesn't fight for something he will accept anything.

As Salaamu Alaikum wrwb.

INDEX

G

H

husband, 32, 33, 37, 56, 57, 59

I

J

K

L

M

man
true, xi, xvii, xviii, xix, xxi, 1, 2, 3, 5, 8, 10, 12, 13, 14, 15, 21, 23, 26, 27, 28, 29, 30, 37, 39, 40, 44, 45, 48, 49, 52, 63, 67, 71, 72, 75
wrath of, xi, xvii, xviii, xix, xxi, 1, 2, 3, 5, 8, 10, 12, 13, 14, 15, 21, 23, 26, 27, 28, 29, 30, 37, 39, 40, 44, 45,

48, 49, 52, 63, 67, 71, 72, 75 Mary, ix, 56, 57, 58, 59
Minnesota, xii, 19, 34, 35, 38, 42, 43,

45, 60, 67, 73
misbehavior, 2
Mississippi, 17, 23, 28, 34, 35, 60 mistakes, 13, 17, 19, 32, 37, 51, 52, 59,

66, 67, 69, 71
Moses, 30
mother, xviii, xix, xx, xxi, 4, 6, 7, 16, 17,

18, 19, 23, 29, 31, 35, 36, 38,
39, 44
Mother's Day, 44, 58
Muslims, xviii, 15

N
Niyaat, 31
P

Panther, 8, 11, 26, 27, 29, 39
Pat, 3
petition, 43
police, xvii, 11, 16, 20, 34, 38, 39, 42,

43, 44, 45, 46, 54, 57, 58, 61 poverty, xv, xviii, 5, 6, 40
pregnancy, 28
prejudice, 16, 38, 43, 54
Price, Danny, 12
pride, 30
probation officer, 20, 32, 33

Q
QUEST, ix, 14
Quran, xix, 14, 15, 44

R

S

GLOSSARY

A

1. Abuse: Physical or emotional mistreatment, including domestic and sexual abuse.
2. Accidental birth: The unplanned birth of a child.
3. African American community: The community of people of African descent living in the United States.
4. Aisha: A name of a person mentioned in the text.
5. Allah: The Arabic word for God, often associated with the Islamic faith.
6. Alzheimer's disease: A neurodegenerative disease that affects memory and cognitive function.
7. Avalon Park: A location or neighborhood mentioned in the text.
8. Ayyub: A name of a person mentioned in the text.

B

1. Beast: A term that may refer to a dangerous or aggressive person.
2. Beauty: The quality of being beautiful or attractive.
3. Ben: A name of a person mentioned in the text.
4. Betrayal: The act of betraying someone's trust or loyalty.
5. Bible: A religious text in Christianity.
6. BM Speedy: A name mentioned in the text.

7. Boo: A name mentioned in the text.

8. Brokenness: A state of being emotionally or mentally broken.

C

1. Cabrini-Green projects: A public housing development in Chicago.

2. Calumet Building: A location mentioned in the text.

3. Catering company: A business that provides catering services.

4. Caucasian methodology: A method or approach associated with Caucasian or white people.

5. Chaos: Disorder and confusion.

6. Charges: Legal accusations or charges against someone.

7. Charity: Voluntary giving to those in need.

8. Chicago: A city in Illinois, USA, and the setting for many events in the text.

9. Children: Young individuals, often referenced in the text.

10. Christianity: A religion based on the teachings of Jesus Christ.

11. Christians: Followers of the Christian faith.

12. Christmas: A Christian holiday celebrating the birth of Jesus Christ.

13. Cocaine: A powerful stimulant drug.

14. Communication: The exchange of information between

individuals.

15. Compassion: Sympathy and concern for the suffering of others.

16. Cosmetology: The study and practice of beauty and cosmetics.

17. Court: A legal institution for hearing cases and dispensing justice.

18. Cousin: A relative, often a child of one's aunt or uncle.

19. CPS (Child Protective Services): A government agency responsible for child welfare.

20. Crip: A reference to a gang member or affiliation with the Crips gang.

D

1. Date rape: Sexual assault that occurs during a date.

2. Daughter: A female child of a parent.

3. Death: The state of no longer being alive.

4. Discord: A lack of agreement or harmony.

5. Dollar Bill: A name mentioned in the text.

6. Domino effect: A chain reaction where one event triggers a series of related events.

E

1. Education: The process of gaining knowledge and skills.

2. Emotions: Feelings or states of mind.

3. Englewood: A neighborhood in Chicago.

4. Ex-husband: A former spouse.

F

1. Failures: Unsuccessful or disappointing outcomes.

2. Faith: Strong belief or trust in something, often of a religious nature.

3. Family: A group of people related by blood or marriage.

4. Father: A male parent.

5. Feds: A colloquial term referring to federal law enforcement agencies.

6. First Lady Deanna: A person mentioned in the text.

7. First loss: The initial experience of losing someone or something.

8. Frank: A name mentioned in the text.

9. Freedom: The state of being free from oppression or constraints.

10. Friendship: A close and supportive relationship between friends.

G

1. Gangs: Organized groups, often involved in illegal activities.

2. Gangster: A member of a criminal organization or a person involved in organized crime.

3. Gangster Disciples (GD): A specific gang mentioned in the

text.

4. God: The supreme being in various religions, including Christianity.

5. Grim Reaper: A symbolic representation of death.

6. Guidance: Advice or direction provided to help someone make decisions.

7. Lack of guidance: A reference to not receiving proper advice or direction.

8. Gunshots: The sound of fired bullets.

H

1. Happiness: A state of well-being and contentment.

2. Hatred: Intense dislike or hostility.

3. Helen: A name mentioned in the text.

4. Hoover, Larry: A person's name mentioned in the text.

5. Hope: A feeling of optimism and expectation.

6. Human rights: Fundamental rights and freedoms to which all humans are entitled.

7. Husband: A male spouse.

I

1. Injustice: Unfair or unjust treatment.

2. Insurance: A financial arrangement for protection against specific risks.

3. Islam: A monotheistic religion based on the teachings of the

Quran.

J

1. Jealousy: Envy or resentment towards others' possessions or achievements.
2. Jessie: A name mentioned in the text.
3. Jimmy D: A name mentioned in the text.
4. Judge: A legal official responsible for presiding over court proceedings.
5. Justice: Fair treatment and the application of the law.
6. JW Marriott: A hotel chain mentioned in the text.

K

1. Kae: A name mentioned in the text.

L

2. Life: The condition of living.
3. Lil C.: A name mentioned in the text.
4. Lil Frank: A name mentioned in the text.
5. Logan Correctional Center: A correctional facility mentioned in the text.
6. Love: Deep affection and care for someone or something.

M

1. Magic: A name mentioned in the text.
2. Maltreatment: Mistreatment or abuse.

3. Man: A reference to a person.

4. Mary: A name mentioned in the text.

5. Minnesota: A state in the United States, mentioned in the text.

6. Misbehavior: Inappropriate behavior or conduct.

7. Mississippi: A state in the United States, mentioned in the text.

8. Mistakes: Errors or wrong decisions.

9. Moses: A biblical figure.

10. Mother: A female parent.

11. Mother's Day: A holiday celebrating mothers.

12. Muslims: Followers of the Islamic faith.

N

1. Niyaat: A name mentioned in the text.

P

2. Panther: A reference to the Black Panther Party or a panther as a symbol.

3. Pat: A name mentioned in the text.

4. Petition: A formal written request or appeal.

5. Police: Law enforcement officers responsible for maintaining order and enforcing the law.

6. Poverty: The state of being extremely poor.

7. Pregnancy: The condition of carrying a developing fetus.

8. Prejudice: Preconceived judgments or biases.

9. Price, Danny: A person mentioned in the text.

10. Pride: A sense of self-respect and satisfaction.

11. Probation officer: A professional supervising individuals on probation.

Q

1. QUEST: A reference to a program or organization.

2. Quran: The holy book of Islam.

R

1. Racism: Discrimination or prejudice based on race.

2. Rape: Sexual assault without consent.

3. Ray, Charles: A reference to the famous musician.

4. Reggie: A name mentioned in the text.

5. Relationship: Connection or association between individuals.

6. Religion: A system of beliefs and practices concerning the divine.

7. Re-Re: A name mentioned in the text.

8. Understanding: The comprehension of information or situations.

9. Responsibilities: Duties or tasks one is responsible for.

10. Righteousness: Moral or ethical correctness.

S

1. Sacrifice: Giving up something valuable for a greater cause.

2. Self-esteem: Confidence and self-worth.

3. Selfishness: A self-centered or egotistical attitude.

4. Self-worth: A sense of one's own value or importance.

5. Shanell: A name mentioned in the text.

6. Sharon: A name mentioned in the text.

7. Shooters: Individuals who shoot or use firearms.

8. Shorty G: A name mentioned in the text.

9. Sister: A female sibling.

10. SKILLS: A reference to skills or abilities.

11. Slavery: The historical practice of owning and exploiting people as property.

12. Son: A male child.

13. Spiritualists: Those who believe in or practice spirituality.

14. Star: A name mentioned in the text.

15. Stepmom: A stepmother, a husband's second wife.

16. Strengths: Positive attributes or qualities.

17. Sunnah: The practices and traditions of the Prophet Muhammad in Islam.

18. Survival: The act of staying alive in difficult circumstances.

T

1. TD: A name mentioned in the text.

2. Ted: A name mentioned in the text.

3. Therapy: Treatment for psychological or emotional issues.

4. Time: The progression of events in chronological order.

5. TJ: A name mentioned in the text.

6. Tone: A name mentioned in the text.

7. Torah: The central reference of the religious Judaic tradition.

8. Trial: A legal process to determine guilt or innocence.

9. Truth: The state of being in accordance with fact or reality.

U

1. Unbreakable bond: A strong and enduring connection that cannot be easily broken.

V

2. Victims: Individuals who have suffered harm or injury.

3. Violence: The use of physical force to cause harm.

W

1. Weaknesses: Personal shortcomings or vulnerabilities.

2. Winndye: A name mentioned in the text.

3. Wisdom: Knowledge and good judgment.

Y

1. YJ: A name mentioned in the text.

2. Young John: A name mentioned in the text.

Z

1. Zeb: A name mentioned in the text.

PHOTO GALLERY

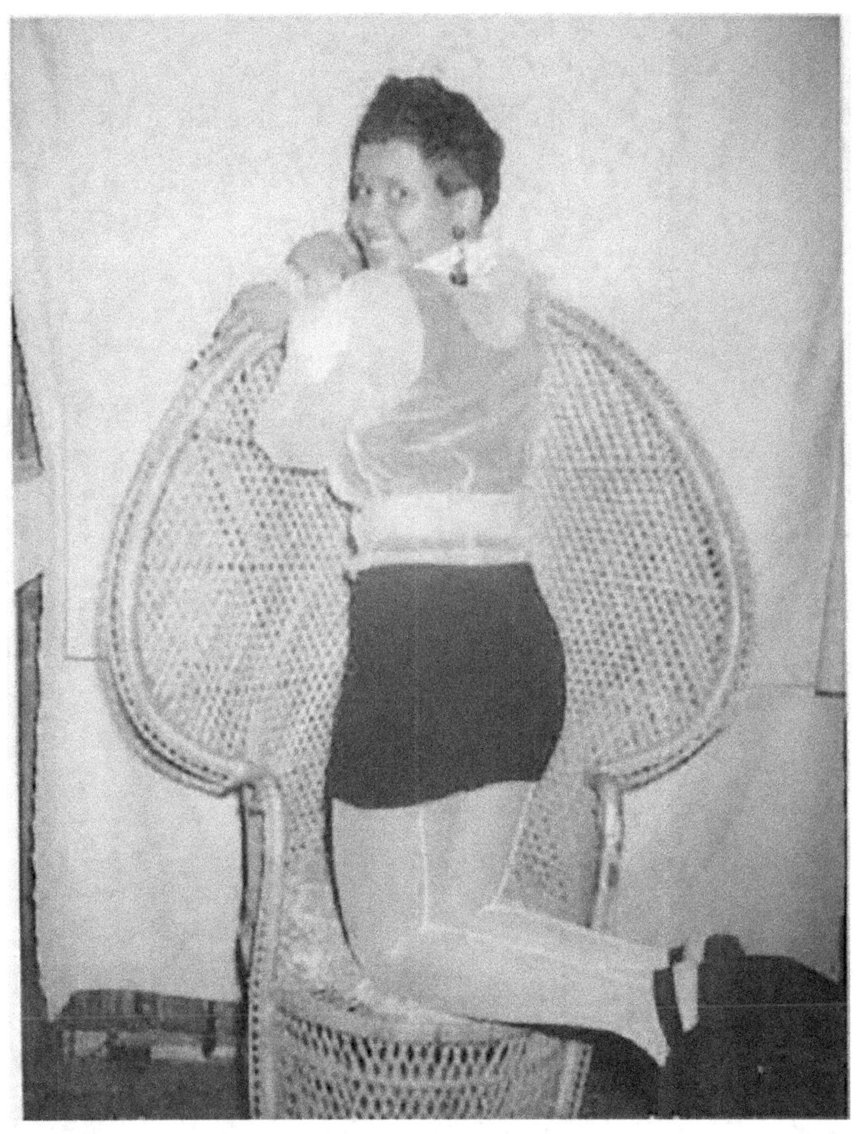

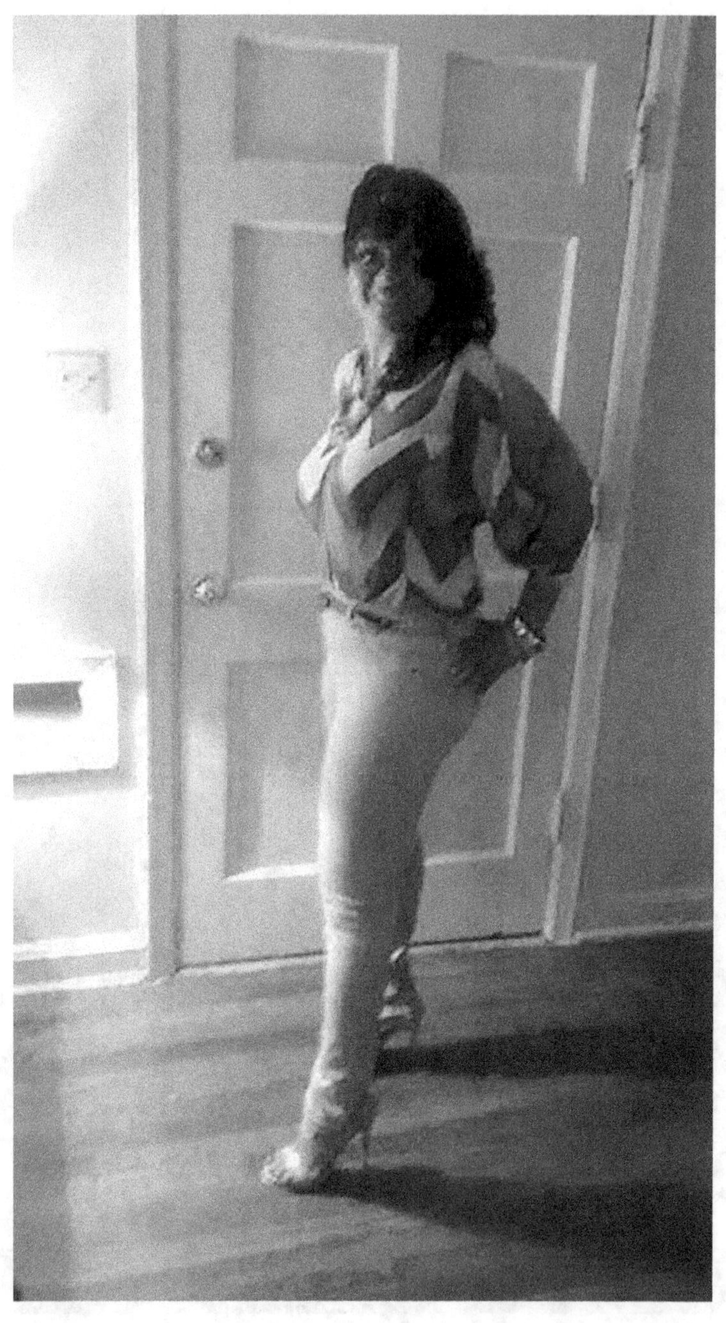

Starte Thomas Runaway Prevention
Program LLC
Healthy Eating
Active Living

BRIDGING
2022 Gala
Presented by BI WORLDWIDE

About The Author

[Details need to be provided]